Jan Michael Joncas

■

Preaching
the Rites of
Christian Initiation

■

Liturgy Training Publications
in cooperation with

The North American Forum on the
Catechumenate

Acknowledgments

The *Forum Essay* series is a cooperative effort of The North American Forum on the Catechumenate and Liturgy Training Publications. The purpose of this series is to provide a forum for exploring issues emerging from the implementation of the order of Christian initiation and from the renewal of the practice of reconciliation in the Roman Catholic Church.

Other titles in the series:

The Role of the Assembly in Christian Initiation
Catherine Vincie

Eucharist as Sacrament of Initiation
Nathan D. Mitchell

On the Rite of Election
Rita Ferrone

Copyright © 1994, Archdiocese of Chicago: Liturgy Training Publications, 1800 North Hermitage Avenue, Chicago IL 60622-1101; 1-800-933-1800, FAX 1-800-933-7094. All rights reserved.

Forum Essays was designed by Mary Bowers and typeset in Futura and Bembo style by Mark Hollopeter. The layout is by Judy Sweetwood, and the cover photograph is by Vicky Grayland. Deborah Bogaert was the production editor. Editors for the series are Victoria M. Tufano (Liturgy Training Publications) and Thomas H. Morris (The North American Forum on the Catechumenate).

Library of Congress Cataloging-in-Publications Data

Joncas, Jan Michael.
    Preaching the rites of Christian initiation/Jan Michael Joncas.
        p. cm. — (Forum Essays; no. 4)
    Includes bibliographical references.
    ISBN 0-929650-79-4: $6.00
    1. Catholic Church. Ordo initiationis Christianae adultorum.
2. Catholic preaching. 3. Initiation rites — Religious aspects — Catholic Church. 4. Catholic Church — Liturgy. 5. Cathechetics — Catholic Church. I. Title. II. Series.
BX2045.I55J66 1994
251 — dc20
                                      94-34932
                                          CIP

CONTENTS

■

Preface

■

Fifteen years ago I was ordained a transitional deacon to serve in the Archdiocese of St. Paul and Minneapolis, Minnesota. During the ceremony, the ordaining bishop told my classmates and me, "Receive the Gospel of Christ, whose herald you now are. Believe what you read, teach what you believe, and practice what you teach." I could not have guessed that in the years since that ceremony preaching would occupy so much of my time and energy.

At the Basilica of St. Mary, an urban parish in downtown Minneapolis where I served my diaconal internship, I learned just how daunting preaching can be in a diverse and transitory community. Fully one half of our congregation each week was a group of one-time visitors to Minnesota's largest city. The other half was a mixture of upper- and middle-class families and singles employed by downtown businesses (including a substantial number of gay and lesbian people), recent immigrants to the

United States (primarily Hmong) and street people. How to bring the gospel to bear on such different human experiences in a single homily was quite a challenge for a twenty-eight-year-old fresh from the seminary!

After presbyteral ordination I spent four years in Maplewood, a middle-class suburb of St. Paul, as associate pastor at the Presentation of the Blessed Virgin Mary parish. There I learned the challenges and rewards of preaching in a fairly stable community. I learned how a preacher can confirm parents' joy at the baptism of their child (even through a background chorus of squeals), can help heal broken spousal and household relationships, can energize believers for social service and political action and can comfort the bereaved at the loss of loved ones. (It was also at Presentation that I learned to modify my liturgical purist's stance as I struggled, more or less successfully, to find a way to yoke "Scout Sunday" with the liturgical calendar!)

My next three-year assignment was as campus minister and education coordinator at the Newman Center at the University of Minnesota, Twin Cities campus. Like many such student ministry centers, this community comprised three distinct subgroups: Catholic undergraduate and graduate students studying at a secular university which was at best bemusedly tolerant, and at worst openly hostile to Catholic Christian faith; university faculty and staff who hoped to find intellectual challenge and emotional support for their vocations as educators; and Catholics alienated, for whatever reason, from their own geographical parishes and searching for an alternative community in which to worship and live out their faith. While at the Newman Center, I became convinced of the value of collaborative approaches to preparing and evaluating preaching, the power of the community's wisdom in "receiving" preaching, and the tensions surrounding both who is authorized to preach in present-day Roman Catholic liturgy and the language that the preacher employs.

For four years after my time at the Newman Center, I lived at Casa Santa Maria while earning a doctorate in liturgical studies at the Pontifical Liturgical Institute at Sant'Anselmo, a Benedictine monastery and school in Rome. I was privileged to hear preaching by graduate-student priests from all over the United States, who reflected not only differences in temperament and theology but characteristic regional variety. While traveling through Europe in those years, I took every chance I could to celebrate liturgy in different rites and languages, coming to appreciate homilies in diverse cultural guises: demonstrative Italian *ferverini;* exquisite French meditations; rigorous German instructions. I also made some stumbling attempts to preach in a language not my own, learning quickly the difference between *Cristo risorto* ("the risen Christ") and *Cristo risotto* ("Christ, the rice casserole")!

Since completing my doctorate, I have enjoyed a full-time assignment as assistant professor of theology at the University of St. Thomas in St. Paul, Minnesota. In addition to my university work, I served for two years as parochial vicar of a four-hundred family parish, St. Cecilia's, and am now weekend "preacher/presider" at the Church of the Immaculate Conception in Columbia Heights, Minnesota.

I do not record these preaching experiences in order to provide verbal snapshots of my travels or to tout my own prowess as a preacher on more than one continent. Rather, I want to let the reader know from the outset some of the factors that have formed my theory and practice of preaching, as well as the limitations I bring to the present task. In all of my pastoral assignments I have been involved at the "grassroots" with Christian initiation. In all of my academic assignments I have both studied and taught the history and present forms of Christian initiation. But I am still quite limited in my insights as a middle-aged, Caucasian, celibate male whose worldview is shaped by the upper Midwestern United States and who came to social and ecclesiastical consciousness in the mid- to late 1960s.

In the following pages I will attempt to define liturgical preaching, sketch what forms liturgical preaching might take in the present rites of Christian initiation for adults in the United States, present a process by which liturgical preaching might be prepared, and list some models of initiation preaching from ancient Christian writers worthy of imitation. By committing these ideas to print, I hope to thank the educators who fired me with love for the church's liturgy when I was still a high school student, the priests and deacons who have modelled liturgical preaching for me, and the ministerial colleagues and parishioners who have, by words of appreciation and criticism, formed me as a preacher.

I would also thank Thomas Morris and The North American Forum on the Catechumenate for inviting me to produce this monograph. Thanks must also be offered to Vicky Tufano and Gabe Huck of Liturgy Training Publications for patiently waiting for the manuscript and guiding the work into print.

This work is dedicated to Father George Szews, pastor of the Newman Parish at the University of Wisconsin at Eau Claire. George is simply the finest preacher I know, one who consistently and fiercely engages the task of transmuting God's word into human discourse. Many of the insights contained herein were honed in our conversations. Even more importantly, his friendship has taught me much about what it means to be a decent human being, a committed Christian and a faithful presbyter.

Soli Deo gloria.

Chapter 1

Toward a Definition of Liturgical Preaching

■

Official church documents, theologians and commentators have all attempted to define the mystery of liturgical preaching. The *General Instruction of the Roman Missal,* for example, describes the eucharistic homily, a privileged form of liturgical preaching, as

> an integral part of the liturgy . . . it is necessary for the nurturing of Christian life. It should develop some point of the readings or of another text from the Ordinary or from the Proper of the Mass of the day, and take into account the mystery being celebrated and the needs proper to the listeners. (#41)

The second edition of the *Introduction to the Lectionary for Mass* expands on this description:

> Through the course of the liturgical year the homily sets forth the mysteries of faith and the standards of the Christian life on the basis of the sacred text. . . . The purpose of the homily at Mass is that the spoken word of God and the liturgy of the eucharist may together become "a proclamation of God's wonderful works in the history of salvation, the mystery of

Christ." Through the readings and the homily Christ's paschal mystery is proclaimed; through the sacrifice of the Mass it becomes present. Moreover Christ himself is also always present and active in the preaching of his church.

Whether the homily explains the biblical word of God proclaimed in the readings or some other texts of the liturgy, it must always lead the community of the faithful to celebrate the eucharist wholeheartedly, "so that they may hold fast in their lives to what they have grasped by their faith." From this living explanation, the word of God proclaimed in the readings and the church's celebration of the day's liturgy will have greater impact. But this demands that the homily be truly the fruit of meditation, carefully prepared, neither too long nor too short, and suited to all present, even children and the uneducated. (#24)

A recent document from the United States National Conference of Catholic Bishops, *Fulfilled in Your Hearing: The Homily in the Sunday Assembly,* reminds us that liturgical preaching

> is not a talk given on the occasion of a liturgical celebration. It is "a part of the liturgy itself." In the eucharistic celebration the homily points to the presence of God in people's lives and then leads a congregation into the eucharist, providing, as it were, the motive for celebrating the eucharist in this time and place. (#60)

Since these official documents seem content to describe rather than define the mystery of liturgical preaching, it might seem foolhardy to attempt a definition. Even so, I have found the following six-fold definition to be useful both in preparing others to preach and as a reminder to myself as preacher of the complexity of the task. Liturgical preaching is

    1) a language event,

    2) contextualized by worship,

    3) inspired by the ritual texts proclaimed and enacted,

    4) addressed to believers,

    5) mediated by preachers,

    6) by which God encounters and transforms God's people.

The remainder of this chapter will be an attempt to unpack this six-fold definition.[1]

A Language Event

The fact that preaching involves human language might seem so obvious that one would not need to underline it. But in fact, the linguistic character of preaching deserves some pondering.

Event First, liturgical preaching is an *event*. Accustomed as we are to reading collections of sermons, we need to remind ourselves that these printed texts are not preaching but the graphic remains of an occurrence of past preaching; somewhat similarly, a musical score is not music but the graphic indication of a potential musical event. I vividly remember a high school teacher of mine illustrating the power of language as event as our sophomore English class embarked on the exploration of American poetry. Without warning, in the middle of a lecture, the teacher singled out one of the students who had been docilely following the lesson and, with glaring eyes skewering the student, said: "Mr. X, I am at the end of my rope. Your constant inattention is both extremely annoying and distracting. I will discuss this with you further after class, but I warn you that I may permanently suspend you if you do not improve!" He then continued with the lesson. My unfortunate comrade blushed to the roots of his hair; the rest of us, incensed at this flagrant abuse of professorial authority, glared back at our teacher. Only gradually did it dawn on us that the teacher was illustrating with a dangerous classroom teaching technique the content of the very poem we had been exploring: "The word lives on/long after its echoes have died away." How powerful must the word-as-event be if it can cause physiological changes in a fifteen-year-old and convert the mood of his friends from passive interest to intense rage to knowing laughter in the space of a few minutes!

Verbal Event   Second, although there have recently been experiments with nonverbal forms of communicating a gospel message, liturgical preaching almost always is a primarily *verbal* event. Some preachers have attempted to communicate a scriptural message through mime, with vivid and striking results, but such embodiment seems more suited to catechetical programs than to formal liturgy. (Of course, preaching in American Sign Language in communities of the deaf and hearing-impaired falls into another category.) Other preachers, doubtless inspired by educational theories noting the potential of multiple modes of communication, have interspersed their preaching with snippets of live or recorded music as a way of reinforcing their message; the powerful rhythmic cadences of much African American preaching especially lends itself to this style of "mixed media" preaching. Some preachers have invited their hearers to gaze upon icons, stained-glass windows or church statuary while their preaching becomes a guided meditation on the religious truths crystallized in these art forms. Still others have treated the architecture of the altar, sanctuary or baptistry as "sermons in stone." There are even preachers who have created slide programs to engage listeners visually during their homilies. But for good or ill, these "mixed media" homilies remain the exception rather than the norm.

Spoken Verbal Event   Third, liturgical preaching is a *spoken* verbal event. Walter Ong has called our attention to the fact that spoken language communicates quite differently than written language does. When one speaks, the hearer cannot re-hear the spoken text unless it is repeated; when one reads, the possibility of going back over an earlier collection of words is always available at the turn of a page and/or with the movement of the eyes.

4

When one reads, one can only extrapolate from the graphic signals to the intended meaning; when one speaks, the tone of voice and various nonverbal behaviors ("para-linguistics") more richly give the auditor an idea of the intended meaning. This is especially important if the text being communicated is intended humorously or ironically (and may also explain why pulpit humor is such a powerful yet dangerous technique).

Although some specialists consider his taxonomy out of date, I find linguist Roman Jakobson's categorization of six dimensions of language helpful when I consider its communicative potential.

Jakobson first identifies a dimension of language used to establish contact between speaker and auditor(s) that he calls *phatic*. A classic example is the greeting exchange in English of "How are you?"/"Fine." Jakobson holds that this exchange does not signal a desire for self-disclosure on the part of either speaker (woe betide the respondent who launches into a lengthy description of his or her physical, mental and emotional well-being in response to this inquiry!). Rather, the purpose of the exchange is simply to establish mutual attention, to make sure that the "linguistic circuit" is operating. (I find it fascinating that the Italian response upon lifting the receiver of a ringing telephone is *"Pronto,"* literally, "Ready!" — a clearly phatic use of language.)

Liturgically, this phatic use of language occurs in liturgical dialogues. Although much ink has been spilled on the cognitive content of the exchange "The Lord be with you"/"And also with you" ("And with your spirit"), it functions less to communicate information about the respective spiritual states of presider and assembly and more to confirm that the liturgical lines of communication are functioning. A similar phatic function was obvious in liturgical practice prior to Vatican II, when preachers began and ended their sermons with a spoken and gestured sign of the cross. This text and gesture really had

5

no cognitive content, but it formally marked the opening and closing of the "preaching circuit." Contemporary preachers must be attentive to their own methods of opening, closing, and checking that the lines of communication are operating during their sermons and homilies.

A second dimension of language, according to Jakobson, is that it is *informative,* presenting the message that the speaker wants to convey. This is probably the use of language that most frequently comes to mind: People generally do not just speak, they speak about something. Their language does not draw attention to itself or to the states of being of speaker and auditor; rather, the language makes present in a certain way the object under discussion. Novice preachers are frequently told that they should be able to present the content of their preaching in a single sentence. This emphasizes the informative character of preaching: that there is a message being proclaimed, that there are certain truth claims being advanced, that there are certain behaviors being promoted and/or denigrated, etc. A danger, however, is that the preacher may so concentrate on the informative content of the preaching, on its message, that she or he neglects the other dimensions of a language event.

Third, an *emotional* dimension of language can be distinguished, according to Jakobson. He uses this term to refer to the clues given by the speaker concerning the speaker's own stance toward the message presented. We all know academic drones who present fascinating material as though it had no vital interest to them, treating their topics with as much relish as reading a phone book. We all know preachers whose body language and vocal production suggest that the message they are proclaiming has no existential claim on them. (I once worked with a very intense workaholic pastor of Germanic background. To watch him lift the consecrated elements, stare off into space and pronounce in an absolute monotone, "This is the Lamb of God who takes away the sins of the world. How happy, *let me repeat that,* how happy are they who are called to the banquet of the Lord," was to experience a liturgical version of the theater of the absurd!) Effective liturgical preaching demands that the preacher's stance toward the message she or he is communicating be coherently and congruently reinforced by both verbal and nonverbal clues.

Fourth, Jakobson delineates a *conative* dimension of language. This means presenting the stance the speaker intends the auditors to take on the basis of the information conveyed. Speakers most frequently invite auditors to share their stance toward the message, but there are occasions when the speaker will promote certain reactions to a particular message. "There is a fire in this building; please remain calm and exit by the rear doorways" can simultaneously convey information about a state of affairs, the speaker's stance toward this state of affairs, and the speaker's intention for the stance the auditors should take toward this state of affairs. It is not enough for preachers to inform their auditors of God's gracious design for the cosmos and their personal appreciation of it without suggesting to them a variety of possible responses to this good news.

Fifth, Jakobson sees that language has a *poetic* dimension, which draws attention to the form of the message as an object of interest in itself. Although some Protestant preaching has been pilloried as "three points and a poem," clear structure and judicious use of rhetorical devices can do much to make the preaching experience aesthetically enriching. Rarely will a preacher compose verse sermons (like the metrical homilies of Ephrem the Syrian or Narsai), but developing the preacher's craft inevitably will lead to an appreciation of the vivid phrase, the arresting image, the appropriate quotation.

Finally, Jakobson classifies a *metalinguistic* dimension of language. Here, language refracts to comment upon itself. Examples of the metalinguistic function are to be found in grammar textbooks and articles on semiotics, but the preacher may also give metalinguistic cues by the use of numerals and connectives or by explicating the range of meaning in biblical words or phrases, thus clarifying the underlying structure of the preaching event.

I contend that good liturgical preaching must be attentive to its character as a spoken verbal event. All six of Jakobson's linguistic functions must be represented in liturgical preaching for it to be effective. I suspect, however, that in most preaching the informative, emotional and conative functions will dominate.

Contextualized by Worship

Verbal language events occur almost constantly whenever human beings are conscious and in the presence of other human beings; but few of these events are preaching. Even fewer verbal language events can be considered liturgical preaching. To narrow the field one must be attentive to the context in which this spoken language event takes place.

Preaching can occur in a variety of contexts. Sometimes the missionary preacher seeks out human beings who have never heard the Christian message about how God has and is acting in Jesus Christ; this foundational type of preaching could be called *evangelical*[2] because its object is the simple proclamation of the gospel leading to conversion to the Christian vision of life. Sometimes the preacher explores with those in Christian formation the practical spiritual consequences of their initial conversion to Christ and his church; this type of preaching might be called *catechetical*,[3] because it seeks to bring to conscious articulation the spiritual experiences of those who are growing in the Christian way of life. Preaching for those who are fully initiated and who live a mature faith might be termed *mystagogical*,[4] a kind of preaching that reinforces the plausibility structures of Christian existence. Notice that all of these types of preaching can occur in many human contexts, both formal and informal, ranging from revival meetings to Bible-study programs to retreat experiences. What characterizes liturgical preaching, however, is not so much the faith-stances of the auditors as the context in which the preaching is done: the Christian assembly at worship. To say that liturgical preaching is contextualized by worship is to assert that it shares in the nature, purpose and goal of Christian worship.

Act of God and Act of the Church In two dense articles from the *Constitution on the Sacred Liturgy,* the Second Vatican Council made a distinctive contribution to our understanding of Christian worship:

> Rightly, then, the liturgy is considered as an exercise of the priestly office of Jesus Christ. In the liturgy, by means of signs perceptible to the senses, human sanctification is signified and brought about in ways proper to each of these signs; in the liturgy the whole public worship is performed by the Mystical Body of Jesus Christ, that is, by the Head and his members. . . . (#7)
>
> The liturgy is the summit toward which the activity of the Church is directed; at the same time it is the fount from which all the Church's power flows. . . . From the liturgy, therefore, particularly the eucharist, grace is poured forth upon us as from a fountain; the liturgy is the source for achieving in the most effective way possible human sanctification and God's glorification, the end to which all the church's other activities are directed. (#10)

For those who share this vision, Christian liturgy by its very nature has a double thrust. On the one hand, it is an act of God in Christ enabling human beings to live in union with God through the Spirit. This might be termed the *descending* nature of worship: God's gracious condescension to alienated humanity, reconstituting and reestablishing a relationship of intimacy with humankind. On the other hand, liturgy is an act of the church in

Christ offering God complete devotion and interceding for the needs of the world through the Spirit. This might be termed the *ascending* nature of worship: redeemed humanity's desire to acknowledge wholeheartedly God's fundamental importance as the source of life, goodness and being itself. It should be clear that the linchpin of Christian worship is Christ, in whom God "bends down" to us and through whom we "rise up" to Jesus' Abba; it should be further clear that such a dynamic is only possible in the Holy Spirit.

To Glorify God and Sanctify the Faithful   The purpose of Christian worship reflects its dual character: according to *Sacrosanctum Concilium,* the Constitution on the Sacred Liturgy, the purpose of sacred liturgy is to "glorify God and sanctify the faithful." On the one hand, it is through the liturgy that the church, as the first fruits of redeemed humanity, offers "glory" to God through Christ in the Spirit. Scripture scholars have pointed out the complexity of the biblical notion of glory *(kabod/ doxa),* but at its core the term is related to "weight" or "heaviness" — that is, "importance." God is glorified when God's foundational importance to the cosmos and to humanity is gratefully acknowledged. Ancient tradition says that the entire nonhuman universe glorifies God simply by existing but that the nobility of humanity is found in its ability to offer "rational worship" *(logikê latreia),* the conscious and self-reflective acknowledgment of God's importance.

On the other hand, it is through the liturgy that the church, as the embodiment of humanity still in need of redemption, is transformed through Christ in the Spirit. Scripture scholars have also pointed out the complexity of the biblical notion of sanctification. In the Eastern Christian traditions, generally, sanctification has been expressed as "divinization" *(theopoiêsis),* the process by which God radically transforms human potential for total union with God. In contrast, the Western Christian traditions have approached sanctification as "justification" *(dikaiosunê),* the process by which God forgives sinners and maintains them in right relationship with God. Thus the church gives glory to God by acknowledging God's foundational importance in creating, sustaining and fulfilling human life and the cosmos. The church is transformed in holiness insofar as its members totally and devotedly give themselves over to the consequences of acknowledging God's glory.

Union with God The goal of Christian worship is complete union with God, individually and communally. Thus the goal of Christian liturgy and the goal of human history converge in the powerful biblical notion of the "Reign of God," the root metaphor that grounds Christian belief and behavior. The goal of Christian worship is to discern the presence of the Reign of God operative in human living, to celebrate that presence in gratitude and acknowledgement, to align the members of the church as conscious participants in God's design for humanity and the universe, and in some way to provide for the participants a genuine glimpse of God's Reign in its fullness.

It should be clear from the foregoing that liturgical preaching as contextualized by worship shares in the liturgy's nature, purpose and goal. Genuine liturgical preaching is Christ's act in the Spirit through the instrumentality of the preacher; it both proclaims to the worshipers the Good News of what God has done, is doing and will do with humanity and the cosmos, and sketches before God the worshipers' patterns of response to God. Genuine liturgical preaching begins and ends in doxology, giving glory to God for God's manifestations in creation, history and scripture, and above all in the life, deeds, death and destiny of Jesus of Nazareth. Liturgical preaching enables the sanctification of the faithful by offering them credible visions of authentic responses to God; it is a spoken language event where the Reign of God can break through personal and communal resistances with transforming spiritual power.

William Willimon succinctly captures this understanding of liturgical preaching when he writes:

> The function of a sermon as a liturgical act is not primarily exhortation, dissemination of information, or instruction on correct doctrine — though these functions may be performed from time to time in sermons. *The primary function is proclamation* — again and again naming the Name, telling the story, keeping time, rehearsing the truth, stating the way things are now that God has come among us, announcing the fact of our adoption as children and heirs. Any ethical payoff from the sermon must derive from this essentially theocentric function. Ethos must not be allowed to precede logos — we do not need a set of sermonic rules for action, we need a story that helps us make sense out of the conflict that circumstances our moral experience, a story as complex and tragic as life itself. Without this sustaining narrative, action is impossible.[5]

Inspired by Ritual Texts Proclaimed and Enacted

There is a joke among pastoral liturgists that the difference between a sermon and a homily is "about twenty minutes." In fact, because both sermons and homilies are spoken language events contextualized by worship, the theoretical distinction between them lies in their inspiration: While a *sermon* is a religious discourse delivered during worship that frequently employs an elevated language register and is on a topic of the preacher's choice, a *homily* is a religious discourse delivered during worship that generally employs a conversational language register and is inspired by the scriptures proclaimed, the liturgical texts enunciated or the festival being celebrated.[6]

One of the most impressive contributions to the liturgical library stemming from the Second Vatican Council's reforms is the *Lectionary for Mass*. This document, which provides normative scriptural selections for Roman Catholic celebrations of the eucharist, has been highly influential; indeed many non–Roman Catholic Christian churches have adopted and adapted the program contained therein. In addition to a three-year cycle for Lord's Day readings and a two-year cycle for weekday readings, the *Lectionary for Mass* also provides unified pericopes for various sacramental celebrations (including the rites of Christian initiation), saints' feasts and ecclesial and civil festivals and needs.

In most cases, liturgical preaching will be inspired by the scriptural selections proclaimed during worship. This is not to say that the scriptures must be searched for a coherent "theme." There is only one theme proclaimed at every liturgical event: God's gracious design for humanity and humanity's response to God through Christ in the Spirit in the church. What varies from worship experience to worship experience is the particular facet of this theme that will be highlighted, a facet that may shine forth from the scriptures proclaimed.

This is also not to say that the preacher's task is merely to instruct the worshipers on the content of the scriptures they hear during worship. Though there is an established tradition of expository preaching, especially among Presbyterian and Reformed preachers, liturgical preaching aims for something different from instruction about the scriptures themselves. The scriptures prescribed and chosen for a given liturgy are intended to inspire the preacher and the assembly to recognize the conformity among the scriptural narratives of God's deeds in the past, the present experience of God's activity and the future promise of the fulfillment of God's promises so that together, preacher and assembly might praise God and be transformed in the process.

It is therefore not surprising that, although they hold pride of place, the inspiration for liturgical preaching is

13

not limited to the scriptural texts proclaimed. It is quite possible for the preacher to inspire worshipers by reflecting on the carefully crafted theology of a collect, the rapturous lyric poetry of a preface or the reassuring familiarity of a frequently proclaimed eucharistic prayer. To point credibly to those events in the world and the worshiping community where God's "spirit changes our hearts: enemies begin to speak to one another, those who were estranged join hands in friendship, and nations speak the way of peace together" (Eucharistic Prayer for Masses of Reconciliation II), is to do liturgical preaching, even though the inspiration for that preaching does not directly come from the scriptures that have been proclaimed at that Mass.

In addition to the proclaimed scriptures and the prescribed liturgical texts, liturgical preaching may also take its inspiration from the season and feast being celebrated. There is an ancient Christian instinct that maps the descending and ascending nature of worship on the very cycles of the cosmos; it sees in the daily sunrise an evocation of Christ's victory over death and in the round of seasons the anticipation, enfleshment, ministry, passion and triumph of God's Reign. Saints' feasts become further instances of the interplay of God's offer and human response, times not only to honor past heroes and heroines but to praise the God who is working the same marvelous transformations in us as we respond to boundless love. There are also personal milestones — anniversaries of birth, baptism, confirmation, marriage, ordination, deaths of loved ones — that mark the ongoing journey of local communities. The preacher who is sensitive to the influence of seasons and feasts in worshipers' lives can help them make the connection between their own lives and the church's ritual prayer.

Fulfilled in Your Hearing succinctly captures this perspective in which liturgical preaching "is not so much on the Scriptures as *from* and *through* them" (#50):

The goal of the liturgical preacher is not to interpret a text of the Bible (as would be the case in teaching a Scripture class) as much as to draw on the texts of the Bible as they are presented in the lectionary to interpret people's lives. To be even more precise, the preacher's purpose will be to turn to these scriptures to interpret people's lives in such a way that they will be able to celebrate eucharist—or be reconciled with God and one another, or be baptized into the Body of Christ, depending on the particular liturgy that is being celebrated. (#52)

Addressed to Believers

If liturgical preaching is a spoken language event contextualized by worship and inspired by ritual texts proclaimed and enacted, it is also addressed to believers: Liturgical preaching is faith speaking *from* and *to* faith.

Liturgical Preaching Is Spoken from Faith   Each of us who has been called by God and church to preach liturgically knows that we are vessels of clay, that the quality of our own faith varies and that we live "in the to and fro/between yes and no" (to use Huub Oosterhuis' wonderful phrase). But we are called to preach the church's faith and not (just) our own foibles. If the worshiping assembly encounters a preacher for any length of time, they will become remarkably aware of his or her hidden vices and buried virtues, even if the preacher avoids directly recounting personal experience in preaching. In my experience, worshipers do not expect perfection from their preachers, whether in the addresses they create, the events in which they deliver them or the lives they lead—but they do expect authenticity.

Liturgical Preaching Is Spoken to Faith   While I admit that there may be some members of the worshiping assembly who are hearing the good news of Christ for the first time, it is my conviction that their

15

numbers will be relatively few and that they do not form the focus of liturgical preaching. (I am presuming a worship context of the Lord's Day assembly, not special occasions such as weddings or funerals, where a significant proportion of the assembly may not share or even have heard the fundamentals of Christian faith.) This is not to downplay the need for evangelical preaching; indeed the *Rite of Christian Initiation of Adults* (RCIA) holds that such preaching is absolutely essential to awakening the first stirrings of faith in unbelievers. But the RCIA positions such preaching *prior* to welcoming them to formal liturgical worship, which serves as the context for catechetical and mystagogical liturgical preaching.

A significant amount of liturgical preaching, especially during celebrations of the rites of Christian initiation, will be *catechetical* in character. Catechetical liturgical preaching consists of empowering worshipers to work through (perhaps for the first time) the implications and consequences of the faith that they have embraced. In the recent past we have treated the word *catechesis* as though it were interchangeable with *religious education*. Such a yoking has at least two implications in pastoral practice: First, liturgical preaching is distorted into religious instruction, the liturgy is distorted into a classroom exercise, and the preacher teaches discrete bits of information rather than evokes the splendor and terror of God's activity in the world. Second, much of our so-called catechetical preaching has been aimed at inculcating religious doctrine into children rather than forming adolescent and adult imaginations in Christian faith. I propose instead that catechetical liturgical preaching takes seriously the worshipers' human experience and attempts to illuminate its meaning in the light of Christian tradition; it seeks to identify and evoke resonances between message proclaimed and life lived so that believers "echo back" the word they have received in their own language and behavior.

In addition to catechesis, liturgical preaching will include a *mystagogical* perspective in which those who believe and have worked through the implications of their faith will be drawn more deeply into that faith, confirmed and strengthened in their encounter with God and socialized under the "sacred canopy" of an explicitly Christian religious world view. I suspect that most mystagogical preaching has been limited to convents, monasteries and parallel forms of the "committed" Christian life. What is a special challenge in preaching at the rites of Christian initiation is the preacher's responsibility to address the catechetical concerns of the initiates while attending mystagogically to the long-term faithful in the assembly.

Mediated by Preachers

If the spoken language event contextualized by worship, inspired by the ritual texts proclaimed and enacted and addressed to believers is to be effective, it must be spoken by someone. *Fulfilled in Your Hearing* proposes that "mediator" may be the most useful self-understanding for a liturgical preacher:

> The person who preaches in the context of the liturgical assembly is . . . a *mediator,* representing both the community and the Lord. . . . The preacher represents this community by voicing its concerns, by naming its demons, and thus enabling it to gain some understanding and control of the evil which afflicts it. He represents the Lord by offering the community another word, a word of healing and pardon, of acceptance and love. . . . The preacher acts as a mediator, making connections between the real lives of people who believe in Jesus Christ but are not always sure what difference faith can make in their lives, and the God who calls us into ever deeper communion with himself and with one another. (#12, 13, 15)

The role of mediator connects the preacher's task with the eternal ministry of Christ. Jesus remains the unique mediator between God and humankind, but the preacher participates in some way in his mediatorship. It is probably for this reason that the *General Instruction of the Roman Missal* notes that "the [eucharistic] homily should ordinarily be given by the priest celebrant" (#42), the one who stands both *in persona ecclesiae* and *in persona Christi capitis ecclesiae.*

On the one hand, the preacher represents the worshiping assembly before God. Such representation is impossible if the preacher has only a superficial understanding of the community from which she or he speaks. The preacher must be attentive to the existential questions of the worshiping assembly: children pitched between exploration and vulnerability, adolescents grappling with identity and intimacy, young adults contending with maintaining Christian ideals in school and work environments that frequently operate from a different vision, middle-aged adults adjusting expectations after youthful dreams are tempered by increasing responsibility and decreasing energy, mature adults finding a niche for themselves in retirement. The preacher must know the stories that individuals and households bring to community worship: the unforeseen falling in love, the unexpected termination of employment, the startling pregnancy, the abrupt bereavement. The preacher must also know the "cover stories" by which the culture frames these individual and household narratives: how popular music, literature, film and television influence the interpretation of existential questions.

Although the quotation from *Fulfilled in Your Hearing* cited earlier suggests that the preacher primarily identifies evils to be confronted in that assembly's narratives and the culture's cover stories, she or he must also be capable of identifying and celebrating how "God is working God's purpose out" in day-to-day activity. At its most intense, rabbinic preaching that puts God on trial, calls God to account and demands that God fulfill the covenant promises positions the preacher as representative of the community before God.

On the other hand, the preacher must not only identify existential questions but also suggest where the divine responses are to be found. Part of the grueling preparation for preaching is developing a habit of mind by which the preacher identifies not only (1) the stories she or he brings as a member of the worshiping assembly and how the cover stories of the culture influence the preacher's thinking, but also (2) what moments of grace and insight have been received from God's Spirit to transform these narratives. The preacher must be free to ask uncomfortable questions, to challenge the common wisdom and to address the worshiping assembly with prophetic authority. Not only does the preacher stand challenging God on behalf of God's people, she or he also stands challenging the people on behalf of God. Norman Neaves captures this tension with telling accuracy:

> How [can one] be prophetic without alienating a congregation[?] . . . How [can one] be prophetic without impairing one's role in pastoral care? In other words, is it possible for one to be a pastor and a prophet at the same time? Can one stand "over against" a congregation in the tradition of a prophet and proclaim the unequivocal "thus saith the Lord" while at the same time being identified with the congregation in the tradition of a priest and mediating the comfort of grace?[7]

I believe that it is not only possible but necessary for preachers to represent both the community before God and God before the community. But this can only be done if preachers are willing to announce God's judgment on their own thoughts and deeds. Preaching that belittles and shames others is not so much prophetic as pathetic, usually revealing not so much God's convicting will as the preacher's unresolved angers and hostilities. It should be remembered that the orientation of liturgical preaching, no matter how thunderously prophetic, is toward doxology, enabling the assembly to praise and thank God and not simply to grovel before God.

A Means by Which God Encounters and Transforms People

Finally, liturgical preaching is closer to an art than a science, more a medium by which the divine reality encounters humankind in all its complexity rather than a neutral mode of analysis oriented toward technological manipulation and control.

Artists know the asceticism demanded by their art. They learn that they are not in control of the well-springs of their creativity but that their art in some mysterious sense "chooses" them. Michelangelo spoke of his activity as a sculptor as recognizing and releasing what was already in the stone. Becoming an artist like Michelangelo demands both attention to technique and greatness of soul. Without refined technique, what is in the stone will never be released; but without greatness of soul, what is in the stone will never be recognized. At the core of all art is contemplation, a disciplined attending to what is real, both in actuality and in potency.

So it is for preachers. We learn that we are not the authors of the word of God but its heralds and its emissaries. In some mysterious way, God's word "chooses" us. Like artists, we must both recognize and release the word enfleshed in our world and in our lives. Without refined homiletic techniques the word will never be released; without greatness of soul we will never be able to hear it in the first place. At the core of all preaching is contemplation, a disciplined displacement of our own egos and agenda so that the word may speak in us. We do not possess the message so much as the message possesses us, for genuine liturgical preaching is first and foremost God's act in Christ empowered by the Spirit mediated through the church; the preacher is God's instrument of encounter.

This sense of preacher as instrument for divine encounter is vividly (some might say garishly) depicted in Susan Howatch's novel *Mystical Paths.* At the climactic scene at the close of the novel, Father Lewis Hall mediates God's healing power by means of the proclaimed word in a prayer service attended by two other Anglican priests, father and son, named Jonathan and Nicholas Darrow. Nicholas narrates the passage:

> Lewis was saying, raising his hands at last to touch us: ". . . and the third text is from [John] chapter eleven. It's the text which so many people nowadays associate with funerals, but that's such an irony as it's the greatest call to life that's ever been uttered. Jesus says — " He broke off, then began again. It was as if he were shifting into a higher gear, and simultaneously, as the timbre of his voice changed, I felt his power lifting us to the very top of his psychic range.
>
> "—Jesus says: 'I am the resurrection, and the life, he that believeth in me, *though he were dead,* YET SHALL HE LIVE — '"
>
> The Force erupted in our midst. . . . There was no sound, but the air was rent from top to bottom as that boundary wall between the possible and the impossible was finally blasted to pieces. I saw Lewis, the channel, shudder under the impact of the explosion, but a second later . . . a brilliant light blinded my eyes . . . and then suddenly the walls collapsed completely so that we were all eternally present in the mind of God, the child raising his tin soldiers from the dead, my mother laughing in the nursery, my father striding through the front door after a day at the Theological College — and with us was not only the Jesus of history, but the Christ of Eternity, holding us together in a moment of triumph over death and victory over darkness. 1949 — 1968 — it didn't matter, it was all one, because the power of Christ was beyond time, no other power could withstand him, and now the darkness generated by my mother's absence was being rolled back and back and back — back until it was utterly extinguished — by that light which was the light of the world — .[8]

While few of us preachers will ever know the use God makes of our stumbling words and feeble gestures (and even fewer of us will possess the "glamorous powers" of psychic awareness ascribed to Lewis and the Darrows in Howatch's novel), we can pray that God will nonetheless make us "instruments of his peace," channels of God's healing power for broken people and a needy world.

Presuming that this working definition of liturgical preaching is somewhat adequate, I will now explore the RCIA's prescriptions in order to clarify the church's expectations for liturgical preaching during the rites of Christian initiation for adults.

Chapter 2

Preaching at the Rites of Christian Initiation

■

The *Rite of Christian Initiation of Adults* (RCIA) structures the initiation process into four continuous periods, punctuated with ritual prayer within each and marking the transition from period to period. This chapter will examine the types of liturgical preaching prescribed for the various stages and steps described by the RCIA.

Period of Evangelization and Precatechumenate

The length and purpose of the first period of initiation, the period of evangelization and the precatechumenate, is clearly delineated in article 7.1 of the RCIA:

> The first period consists of inquiry on the part of the candidates and of evangelization and the precatechumenate on the part of the church. It ends with the rite of acceptance into the order of catechumens.

23

Furth.. ..r articles specify the preaching focus of this period:

It is a time of evangelization: faithfully and constantly the living God is proclaimed and Jesus Christ whom he sent for the salvation of all. Thus those who are not yet Christians, their hearts opened by the Holy Spirit, may believe and be freely converted to the Lord and commit themselves sincerely to him. (#36)

From evangelization, completed with the help of God, come the faith and initial conversion that cause a person to feel called away from sin and drawn into the mystery of God's love. The whole period of the precatechumenate is set aside for this evangelization, so that the genuine will to follow Christ and to seek baptism may mature. (#37)

During this period, priests and deacons, catechists and other laypersons are to give the candidates a suitable explanation of the gospel. (#38)

The implications of these prescriptions for the liturgical preacher are far-reaching.

First, the auditors are called *inquirers,* those who are "not yet Christians." Thus the RCIA presumes them to be people who have not heard the gospel or been baptized into a Christian denomination. I divide inquirers into three categories based on their prior religious stance.

Jews and Muslims form the first category. They already believe that a single God exists, that God intervenes in history, that God makes moral demands on those whom God elects and that certain written documents *(TaNaK or Qu'ran)* give access to God's self-disclosure to humanity. Theists form the second category. They range from worshipers of Brahman or Shiva to the practitioners of New Age spirituality. In many cases these inquirers bring a profound sense of spiritual experience and even disciplined meditation techniques to their inquiry. They are hoping to discover how Christian belief compares with (and perhaps brings to fulfillment) their spiritual path. The third category comprises agnostics and atheists. Frequently some experience of delight (e.g., falling in love with and preparing to wed a Roman Catholic) or difficulty (e.g., coming to trust a Higher Power in recovering from addictions) prompts them to reexamine their stance toward God's existence and character.

Second, the preacher's evangelizing task is to proclaim Jesus as God's response to humanity's deepest longings. For inquirers of Jewish background, Jesus' own heritage as a Jew, his passion for the God of the Abrahamic, Sinaitic and Davidic covenants, and his role as a prophetic critic of his religious heritage may serve as a point of entry for evangelizing. For inquirers of Islamic heritage, Jesus' devotion to God's sovereignty and God's Reign, even to the point of giving his own life, could gain a hearing for his religious claims. For theists, Jesus can be presented as a religious teacher of surpassing wisdom whose doctrine deserves a hearing alongside the spiritual masters whom the inquirers have already explored. For agnostics and atheists Jesus can be portrayed as such an attractive and authentic human being as to invite consideration of his religious claims. In any case, the preacher should stick to what is basic and distinctive in the Christian worldview: the life, teaching, death and destiny of Jesus.

Third, the effectiveness of evangelical preaching according to the RCIA can be assessed by attending to certain criteria. Fundamental to Christian conversion is a personal commitment to Jesus. (Such personal commitment seems to be one of the marks that distinguishes disciples [*mathêtês*] of Jesus from the disciples of other New Testament figures such as John the Baptizer, Paul or the Pharisees.) While full-fledged faith in Jesus as Lord and Savior may not yet be in evidence, those effectively touched by evangelical preaching must view Jesus as something more than a misguided Jewish fanatic, a noble martyr killed for a cause or a spiritual teacher taking his place alongside other gurus. Fundamental faith in Jesus will manifest itself in at least two ways: Those passing from the stage of inquirer to catechumen will evidence a change in their moral thinking and behavior and will be drawn to personal and communal prayer.

Fourth, evangelical preaching is generally *not* liturgical preaching as we have described it in chapter one. Although evangelical preaching is a language event mediated by preachers by which God encounters and transforms people, it is not usually contextualized by worship, inspired by ritual texts proclaimed and enacted, or addressed to those who already believe as Christians. Fifth, evangelical preaching is not limited to those in holy orders. While bishops, presbyters and deacons may be the privileged preachers of the liturgical homily, catechists and other lay people seem especially effective as evangelizers. Their preaching should involve not only information about Jesus correlated with the inquirers' circumstances but personal witness about how life in Jesus affects them.

These reflections on preaching during the period of evangelization and the precatechumenate can be crowned with Paul VI's wise words in his apostolic exhortation on evangelization in the modern world, *Evangelii nuntiandi,* issued on 8 December 1975:

> Preaching that proclaims the gospel can take many forms, which a burning zeal for souls will suggest and vary almost infinitely. In fact there are innumerable events and situations in human life that offer the opportunity for a discreet but incisive statement of what the Lord wishes to say to this or that particular circumstance. A person simply needs a genuine spiritual sensitivity to read God's message in the events of life. . . . This kind of preaching certainly has a particular role in evangelization, because it expresses the sacred minister's profound faith and is suffused with love. . . . But it must be simple, clear, direct, well adapted, profoundly dependent on the gospel, faithful to the magisterium, animated by the balanced apostolic ardor that is of its essence, full of hope, fostering belief and productive of peace and unity.[1]

Rite of Acceptance into the Order of Catechumens

Article 41 of the RCIA sketches the dual purpose of the rite of acceptance, by which the period of evangelization reaches its completion and the period of the catechumenate opens:

> Assembling publicly for the first time, the candidates who have completed the period of the precatechumenate declare their intention to the church and the church in turn, carrying out its apostolic mission, accepts them as persons who intend to become its members.

Thus the event being celebrated is the fruit of mutual discernment: Those who have been evangelized discern in the community of the faithful the Spirit-filled presence of Christ mediating the living God, and the community discerns in those who have been evangelized authentic seekers after fullness of life in Christ. The rite of acceptance is a rite of separation. The inquirers become liminal, entering a "betwixt and between" stage in which they are neither simply gathering information any longer, nor have they become fully committed Christians, but they have publicly declared their intention to join the Christian community. Its ritual structure (assembling at the threshold *[limen]* of the church, covenant-making between candidates and the faithful through ritual dialogues, signing the candidates with Christ's cross, processing into the house of the church, listening to God's word in scripture proclaimed and preached, praying for and over the catechumens and sending them forth) clearly symbolizes the catechumens' special place within and yet separate from the mass of the Christian faithful.

Because the rite of acceptance is not tied to a particular Sunday or weekday eucharistic celebration, article 62 notes that "the readings may be chosen from any of the readings in the *Lectionary for Mass* that are suited to the new catechumens." However, the set of scriptures appointed for the rite of acceptance (*Lectionary for Mass,*

743) provides an exquisite foundation for catechetical preaching. (Note that the lectionary provides one Hebrew scripture proclamation, one responsorial psalm, a verse before the gospel and one gospel proclamation; does this suggest that the rite of acceptance should be celebrated on a weekday?)

Genesis 12:1 – 4a, recounting God's call to Abraham to leave the land of his kin and Abraham's response, mirrors the catechumens' own spiritual situation: God has called them on a journey of faith and they have publicly committed themselves to the journey. A preacher might want to highlight the election/command/promise dynamic in the reading as well as the fact that the catechumens' spiritual journey, like Abraham's ("and Lot went with him"), will be communal in character. The first suggested refrain for the responsorial psalm (33:4 – 5, 12 – 13, 18 – 19, 20 and 22), "Happy the people the Lord has chosen to be his own," seems especially appropriate. Basing his reflections on the psalm text, a preacher might stress that the Lord who elects and promises is trustworthy both in word and works; he might give concrete examples and personal testimony, and call the catechumens and faithful to wait on the Lord, in whom they have put their hope.

John 1:35 – 42 narrates how two disciples of John the Baptizer shift their allegiance from John and his message to Jesus, how Jesus personally invites them to discover his lifestyle, how those who have faith in Jesus bring others to encounter Jesus and how a change in name signifies a transformation in being. While any of these elements could inspire a preacher, I would highlight the dialogue between Jesus and the former disciples of John as an outline of the catechumenate: 1) "What are you looking for?" is the foundational question for inquirers; 2) "Rabbi, where do you abide?" acknowledges Jesus as the spiritual guide ("Teacher") whose teaching during the catechumenate will instruct them on how to abide in God by abiding in him; and 3) "Come and see" points to the invitation the faithful make to the catechumens in Jesus' name for the duration of their catechumenate — to move from isolation into the Christian assembly and to begin to share the Christian worldview. The verse before the gospel might make a powerful conclusion to the preaching: "We have found the Messiah: Jesus Christ, who brings us truth and grace."

The ritual texts and ceremonies also provide sources for preaching at the rite of acceptance: fleshing out the opening dialogue on how Christ calls us each by name, how the church mediates faith in Christ and how faith leads to eternal life; reflecting on how the signing of the senses engages the catechumens in the paschal mystery; or presenting the catechumenate as a journey ritualized by being welcomed at the threshold of the church, honored in its midst and sent out to ponder God's action in their lives.

Period of the Catechumenate

The length and purpose of the second period described by the RCIA, the catechumenate proper, resounds in article 7.2:

> The second period, which begins with the rite of acceptance into the order of catechumens and may last for several years, includes catechesis and the rites connected with catechesis. It comes to an end on the day of election.

Additional articles specify the preaching focus of this period:

> A suitable catechesis is provided by priests or deacons, or by catechists and others of the faithful, planned to be gradual and complete in its coverage, accommodated to the liturgical year and solidly supported by celebrations of the word. This catechesis leads the catechumens not only to an appropriate acquaintance with dogmas and precepts but also to a profound sense of the mystery of salvation in which they desire to participate. (#75.1)

29

> The church, like a mother, helps the catechumens on their journey by means of suitable liturgical rites, which purify the catechumens little by little and strengthen them with God's blessing. Celebrations of the word of God are arranged for their benefit, and at Mass they may also take part with the faithful in the liturgy of the word, thus better preparing themselves for their eventual participation in the liturgy of the eucharist. (#75.3)

Celebrations of the Word of God Article 81 of the RCIA intimates that the nature of initiation preaching during the catechumenate will be mixed. Some, like the preaching during the period of evangelization and the precatechumenate, will be nonliturgical, while some will be genuine liturgical preaching, i.e., contextualized by worship, inspired by the ritual texts proclaimed and enacted, and addressed to those of genuine (though rudimentary) faith.

> During the period of the catechumenate there should be celebrations of the word of God that accord with the liturgical season and that contribute to the instruction of the catechumens and the needs of the community. These celebrations of the word are: first, celebrations held especially for the catechumens; second, participation in the liturgy of the word at the Sunday Mass; third, celebrations held in connection with catechetical instruction.

Note that the RCIA distinguishes between "celebrations of the word" and the eucharistic "liturgy of the word": the former presumably would include preaching by lay leaders of community prayer, while the latter would reserve preaching to the ordained.

It is difficult to give concrete suggestions for initiation preaching during the catechumenal period because there are no appointed readings for specifically catechumenal celebrations or catechetical events; to comment on all of the readings of the liturgy of the word at Sunday eucharist would far exceed the limits of this monograph. Preachers can use the criteria of article 82 as a checklist for their initiation preaching during the catechumenate:

The special celebrations of the word of God arranged for the benefit of the catechumens have as their main purpose: (1) to implant in their hearts the teaching they are receiving: for example, the morality characteristic of the New Testament, the forgiving of injuries and insults, a sense of sin and repentance, the duties Christians must carry out in the world; (2) to give them instruction and experience in the different aspects and ways of prayer; (3) to explain to them the signs, celebrations and seasons of the liturgy; (4) to prepare them gradually to enter the worship assembly of the entire community.

Some initiation preaching thus will consist of moral exhortation; if during the period of evangelization the Christian vision of reality was proclaimed, catechetical preaching can now explore the behavioral implications of assuming the Christian story. Other initiation preaching will introduce catechumens to various practices of Christian prayer: The preacher will both describe and model adoration, thanksgiving, confession, intercession and petitionary prayer, perhaps even exploring meditative and contemplative dimensions of the human-divine interchange individually and in groups. The symbolic languages of the liturgy also will be explored in initiation preaching; this is not "mystagogic" preaching because the catechumens have not yet taken active roles in the Christian liturgy as baptized members. But it does invite contemplative engagement with the Christian structuring of life (birth, excommunication and reconciliation, marriage, vocation, sickness, death), time (daily, weekly, yearly rituals) and space (postures, gestures, architecture, artifacts, color codes). The peculiar practices of the local worship assembly will also be explained: ethnic customs, household traditions, important festivals. Preachers must strive to find a balance among these various topics during the course of the catechumenate.

Special celebrations of the word during the catechumenate may conclude with a variety of ritual gestures: minor exorcisms, blessings and/or anointings. On occasion, preachers might want to reflect on: the character of the minor exorcisms as gentle requests that God assist and accompany catechumens in times of community tension, of recognition of personal sin and of grappling with structural evils; the power of blessings to mediate God's presence with the graces of courage, joy and peace to the catechumens; and the anointings as ritual acts honoring, healing, soothing and strengthening those under instruction.

Rite of Sending Catechumens for Election. An optional rite for sending catechumens to the cathedral church or some other diocesan regional center for the rite of election appears in the edition of the RCIA approved in 1988 for use in the dioceses of the United States. Article 107 presents the pastoral concerns that led to the development of this rite:

> As the focal point of the church's concern for the catechumens, admission to election belongs to the bishop who is usually its presiding celebrant. It is within the parish community, however, that the preliminary judgment is made concerning the catechumens' state of formation and progress. This rite offers that local community the opportunity to express its approval of the catechumens and to send them forth to the celebration assured of the parish's care and support.

Three practical concerns influence the kind of preaching to be done at this rite. First, will the rite be celebrated at the parish eucharist on the First Sunday of Lent, on Ash Wednesday, or on some other (lenten) weekday prior to the date of the diocesan celebration of the rite of election? (If it is celebrated on the First Sunday of Lent, the readings proclaimed may duplicate those pronounced at the rite of election.) Second, will the rite of sending be celebrated during the course of a eucharist or as part of a celebration of the word of God? If the former, it is presumed that the ordained minister will preside and preach, but if the latter, a lay minister (such as a pastoral life coordinator) might preside and preach. Third, if both catechumens and baptized candidates for full communion with the Roman Catholic church are sent for election and recognition, respectively, by the bishop, will the parish community celebrate individual rites of sending for each group (perhaps on Ash Wednesday for the candidates and on the First Sunday of Lent for the catechumens) or a combined rite for both?

Depending on the ceremonies performed during this rite, the preacher might want to highlight the calling of the catechumens by name, the testimony of the godparents/sponsors as witness to what God is doing in the lives of the catechumens, or the covenantal implications of the signing of the Book of the Elect (cf. the biblical imagery of names inscribed in the "Book of Life" [Revelations 21:27]).

These reflections on preaching during the catechumenate can be summarized in John Paul II's words concerning the homily from his apostolic exhortation on catechesis in our time, *Catechesi tradendae,* issued on 16 October 1979:

> Respecting the specific nature and proper cadence of this setting, the homily takes up again the journey of faith put forward by catechesis and brings it to its natural fulfillment. At the same time it encourages the Lord's disciples to begin anew each day their spiritual journey in truth, adoration and thanksgiving. Accordingly, one can say that catechetical teaching too finds its source and fulfillment in the eucharist, within the whole circle of the liturgical year. Preaching, centered upon the Bible texts, must then in its own way make it possible to familiarize the faithful with the whole of the mysteries of faith and with the norms of Christian living. Much attention must be given to the homily: it should be neither too long nor too short; it should always be carefully prepared, rich in substance and adapted to the hearers and reserved to ordained ministers. The homily should have its place not only in every Sunday and feast-day eucharist but also in the celebration of baptisms, penitential liturgies, marriages and funerals. This is one of the benefits of the liturgical renewal.[2]

Rite of Election

Article 118 of the RCIA delineates the meaning and placement of the rite of election or enrollment of names:

> The second step in Christian initiation is the liturgical rite called both election and the enrollment of names, which closes the period of the catechumenate proper, that is, the lengthy period of formation of the catechumens' minds and hearts. The celebration of the rite of election, which usually coincides with the opening of Lent, also marks the beginning of the period of final, more intense preparation for the sacraments of initiation, during which the elect will be encouraged to follow Christ with greater generosity.
>
> At this second step, on the basis of the testimony of godparents and catechists and of the catechumens' reaffirmation of their intention, the church judges their state of readiness and decides on their advancement toward the sacraments of initiation. Thus the church makes its "election," that is, the choice and admission of those catechumens who have the dispositions that make them fit to take part, at the next major celebration, in the sacraments of initiation.
>
> This step is called election because the acceptance made by the church is founded on the election by God, in whose name the church acts. The step is also called the enrollment of names because as a pledge of fidelity the candidates inscribe their names in the book that lists those who have been chosen for initiation. (#119)

Like the rite of acceptance into the order of catechumens, the rite of election is founded on mutual discernment. The catechumens, after a time of input and reflection possibly lasting several years, "elect" to complete their Christian initiation by presenting themselves for baptism. The church in turn "elects" certain catechumens for full initiation because it has discerned God's salvific choice of these individuals for complete life in Christ. Article 128 specifies the preaching focus for this event:

> The rite is celebrated within Mass, after the homily, and should be celebrated within the Mass of the First Sunday of Lent. If, for pastoral reasons, the rite is celebrated on a different day, the texts and the readings of the ritual Mass "Christian Initiation: Election or Enrollment of Names" may always

be used. When the Mass of the day is celebrated and its read-ings are not suitable, the readings are those given for the First Sunday of Lent or others may be chosen from elsewhere in the lectionary.

When celebrated outside Mass, the rite takes place after the readings and the homily and is concluded with the dismissal of both the elect and the faithful.

Lectionary for Mass, 744, indicates that when the rite of election is celebrated on the First Sunday of Lent the readings for that Sunday of Years A, B or C may be cho-sen; if the rite is celebrated on a (lenten) weekday when the readings seem less appropriate, these Sunday readings may be substituted or other suitable readings could be chosen. As was noted earlier, when the rite of sending is celebrated as part of the parish eucharist on the First Sunday of Lent, the readings appointed for that particu-lar Sunday will have already been proclaimed and preached. Using the same texts may tie together parish and diocesan celebrations. Some may prefer, however, to combat ritual redundancy by selecting one of the sets of readings from the same Sunday of a different year.

Although it does not demand it, the RCIA clearly pre-fers that the rite of election be celebrated as a diocesan liturgy presided over by the bishop, who then has pri-mary responsibility for preaching at this event:

> After the readings . . . the bishop, or the celebrant who acts as delegate of the bishop, gives the homily. This should be suited to the actual situation and should address not just the cate-chumens but the entire community of the faithful, so that all will be encouraged to give good example and to accompany the elect along the path of the paschal mystery. (#129)

The scriptures appointed for the First Sunday of Lent in Year A (*Lectionary for Mass,* 22) confront the elect and the faithful alike with the reality of sin and the divine offer of salvation. Genesis 2:7 – 9; 3:1 – 7 recounts the Fall narrative in the mythological terms of the Yahwist cre-ation account. Rather than concentrating on the imagi-native details of the story, the preacher may want to highlight its central theological truths: that humanity occupies a special place in God's creation, that humanity's choices have alienated humanity from God, and that neither God nor fate can be blamed for humanity's present condition.

The responsorial psalm (51:3 – 4, 5 – 6, 12 – 13, 14, 17), one of the seven penitential psalms, profoundly complements the Genesis reading by acknowledging how the sin of the world is personally confirmed by every individual's sins; its suggested refrain, "Be merciful, O Lord, for we have sinned" brilliantly combines personal and communal recognition of the human condition and God's power to transform it.

Of the two versions of the New Testament letter appointed for proclamation (Romans 5:12 – 19 or 5:12, 17 – 19), the shorter more clearly presents the Pauline contrast between the old and the new Adam. The preacher could emphasize Jesus as God's redeeming gift to humanity over and above the initial gift of creation.

But preaching based on the temptation narrative in Matthew 4:1 – 11 would allow the homilist to present the period of purification and enlightenment as the imitation of Christ, a time for those committed to baptism to spend forty days and nights in a spiritual desert, allowing the power of Christ to help them overcome urges to prize earthly nourishment over spiritual sustenance, magical manipulation over religious trust, and social prestige to authentic creaturehood.

In Year B the scripture readings appointed for the First Sunday of Lent (*Lectionary for Mass,* 23) exhibit a clear baptismal focus. Genesis 9:8 – 15, the Priestly version of God's covenant with Noah, challenges the preacher to explore the universality of God's concern (the covenant is made not only with Israel but with the whole human race), God's will to save rather than to destroy, and how invisible covenant relationships with God are manifest in visible signs (a rainbow in the covenant with Noah, circumcision in the covenant with Abraham, Torah in the covenant with Moses, progeny in the covenant with David, and baptism and eucharist in the covenant established in Christ).

The responsorial psalm (25:4–5, 6–7, 8–9) underscores the behavioral consequences of the covenant thematic announced in the Genesis reading; its suggested refrain, "Your ways, O Lord, are love and truth, to those who keep your covenant," reminds the elect and the faithful that this is not a covenant between equal parties but that the sovereign God is the guarantor of the covenant promises and has the right to impose covenant stipulations.

1 Peter 3:18–22 emphasizes the connections between Noah's flood and Christian baptism: Noah and his family are "saved through water" (the water being both a hostile element which might have drowned them and the means by which the ark floated to safety) just as the passage through the waters of baptism is death to the powers hostile to Christ and is the means of rescue for the faithful; the preacher might also draw the parallel between the eight persons brought to safety in the ark and the Christian community in its voyage to the Reign of God.

Unlike the temptation gospels in Years A and C, Mark 1:12–15 simply records the fact of Jesus' temptation without narrating individual events. The preacher might want to concentrate on the summary of Jesus' preaching found in verses 14–15, declaring that the time of fulfillment and the reign of God have been inaugurated in the life, death and resurrection of Jesus and that the appropriate response from the elect and the faithful is conversion *(metanoia)* to the way of Christ and belief in him — conversion and belief that are actualized in adult Christian initiation.

The scriptures appointed for the First Sunday of Lent in Year C (*Lectionary for Mass*, 24) are centered around the notion of "confession," not so much of sin as of faith.

37

Deuteronomy 26:4 – 10, containing one of the most ancient fragments of oral tradition in the Bible, represents a central confession of faith for Jews: that the Exodus of a marginalized group of laborers from conditions of slavery in Egypt was not simply a human escape but a manifestation of God's "mighty hand and outstretched arm" liberating the oppressed.

The responsorial psalm (91:1 – 2, 10 – 11, 12 – 13, 14 – 15) seems to have been chosen for its connection with the gospel reading, but verses 14 – 15 declare that God promises liberation for all who cling to God and acknowledge his name; its suggested refrain, "Be with me, Lord, when I am in trouble," can tie together Jesus' trusting stance toward his Abba-God, the plea of the elect during this period of purification and the petition of the faithful to Christ during Lent.

Romans 10:8 – 13 parallels the Jewish faith-confession of the Deuteronomy reading with the classic Christian confession: "Jesus is Lord!"; the preacher might want to compare and contrast the promises, identities and destinies generated by these two confessions.

Luke 4:1 – 13 narrates three temptations of Jesus at the conclusion of his forty-day fast; the preacher might want to emphasize that this narrative reaches its climax in Jerusalem, the city where Jesus will publicly confess his faith in God even to death on the cross rather than attempt to manipulate the divine will for his own benefit. Both the elect and the faithful can be encouraged to emulate their Lord by public confession of their faith in him no matter what the cost.

The homilist might also choose to preach on the other ritual texts and ceremonies employed during the rite of election. The testimony of the godparents, the ceremony of inscribing or calling out names, or the placing of godparents' hands on the elect while the community intercedes for them and the presider prays over them could all serve as sources for homiletic reflection.

Period of Purification and Enlightenment

The length and purpose of the third stage of initiation, the period of purification and enlightenment, appears in article 7.3:

> The third and much shorter period, which follows the rite of election, ordinarily coincides with the lenten preparation for the Easter celebration and the sacraments of initiation. It is a time of purification and enlightenment and includes the celebration of the rites belonging to this period.

The preaching focus of this period emerges in further articles:

> In the liturgy and liturgical catechesis of Lent the reminder of baptism already received or the preparation for its reception, as well as the theme of repentance, renew the entire community along with those being prepared to celebrate the paschal mystery, in which each of the elect will share through the sacraments of initiation. For both the elect and the local community, therefore, the lenten season is a time for spiritual recollection in preparation for the celebration of the paschal mystery. (#138)
>
> This is a period of more intense spiritual preparation, consisting more in interior reflection than in catechetical instruction, and is intended to purify the minds and hearts of the elect as they search their own consciences and do penance. This period is intended as well to enlighten the minds and hearts of the elect with a deeper knowledge of Christ the Savior. (#139)

Notice the shift in focus that occurs: It moves from "catechetical instruction" to "interior reflection." Thus, the initiation preaching that will take place during this period will exhibit a different character than the preaching we saw during the preceding stage. The period of purification and enlightenment is the most densely structured of all the stages of initiation; here I will treat the implications for preaching of the scrutinies, the presentations and the optional Holy Saturday rites that are celebrated during this period.

Scrutinies   Articles 141 and 143 of the RCIA present the progressive character of the three scrutinies celebrated during the period of purification and enlightenment:

> The scrutinies, which are solemnly celebrated on Sundays and are reinforced by an exorcism, are rites for self-searching and repentance and have above all a spiritual purpose. The scrutinies are meant to uncover, then heal all that is weak, defective, or sinful in the hearts of the elect; to bring out, then strengthen all that is upright, strong and good. For the scrutinies are celebrated in order to deliver the elect from the power of sin and Satan, to protect them against temptation and to give them strength in Christ, who is the way, the truth and the life. These rites, therefore, should complete the conversion of the elect and deepen their resolve to hold fast to Christ and to carry out their decision to love God above all.
>
> In order to inspire in the elect a desire for purification and redemption by Christ, three scrutinies are celebrated. By this means, first of all, the elect are instructed gradually about the mystery of sin, from which the whole world and every person longs to be delivered and thus saved from its present and future consequences. Second, their spirit is filled with Christ the Redeemer, who is the living water (gospel of the Samaritan woman in the first scrutiny), the light of the world (gospel of the man born blind in the second scrutiny), the resurrection and the life (gospel of Lazarus in the third scrutiny). From the first to the final scrutiny the elect should progress in their perception of sin and their desire for salvation.

The RCIA exhibits a distinct preference that preaching at the scrutinies be grounded in the readings and not simply in the ritual texts and ceremonies:

> After the readings and guided by them, the celebrant explains in the homily the meaning of the . . . scrutiny in the light of the lenten journey and of the spiritual journey of the elect. (#151, 165, 172)

First Scrutiny   The readings appointed for the Third Sunday of Lent in Year A (*Lectionary for Mass,* 28) form the scriptural context for the first scrutiny. *Lectionary for Mass,* 745, indicates that whenever the first scrutiny is celebrated these readings and chants are to be used (i.e., even when the scrutiny might be celebrated on a weekday or on a Sunday in another cycle). Baptismal thematics mark all the scriptural proclamations; symbols clustering around water provide a strong imaginative challenge to the preacher.

Exodus 17:3–7 narrates the incident at Massah and Meribah ("Testing and Quarrel") in which God through Moses provides water to sustain the grumbling Hebrews in their desert journey from slavery in Egypt to freedom in the promised land. While some patristic commentators (e.g., John Chrysostom, Ambrose) see a prefigurement of the eucharistic meal in this water conjoined with manna, contemporary preachers would most likely follow Cyprian of Carthage in interpreting this passage as a type of baptism.

The responsorial psalm (95:1–2, 6–7, 8–9), familiar as an invitatory to those who pray the liturgy of the hours, does not underscore baptismal thematics so much as it encourages perseverance when the faith journey becomes difficult; its suggested refrain, "If today you hear his voice, harden not your hearts," might be appropriately directed to the faithful as well as to the elect.

Romans 5:1–2, 5–8 is an extraordinarily rich theological meditation on our justification by faith in the saving act of Christ; the homilist might want to connect the metaphor of the love of God "poured out" in human hearts through the Holy Spirit with the water imagery in the Exodus and John readings and the baptismal ceremony itself.

John 4:5–42, the narrative of Jesus' encounter with the Samaritan woman at Jacob's well, provides an embarrassment of riches for the preacher. Some preachers might want to explore the shifts in titles given to Jesus during the narrative (Jew, sir, prophet, Messiah, Savior of the world) as a record of growth in faith; others might concentrate on the different relations to Jesus represented by the Samaritan woman, Jesus' disciples and the Samaritan townspeople as analogs to the various relations to Jesus found in both church and world. The strongest initiation theme might be found in commenting on Jesus' promise that the water he gives will become a fountain within, leaping up to provide eternal life; the preacher could anticipate the Johannine passion narrative proclaimed on Good Friday in which the water flowing from the crucified Jesus' side connects to this promised fountain of life, sacramentally actualized in baptism.

Second Scrutiny   The second scrutiny is celebrated with the readings appointed for the Fourth Sunday of Lent in Year A (*Lectionary for Mass,* 31). *Lectionary for Mass,* 746, directs that these readings are to be used even when the second scrutiny is celebrated on a weekday or a Sunday in another cycle. The symbols in this set of readings group around light and darkness, leading to the proclamation that Jesus is the light of the world.

1 Samuel 16:1, 6 – 7, 10 – 13, with its narrative of the anointing of David (the least likely candidate) as king of Israel, has been selected (like the other Sunday Old Testament readings for Lent) to recount the high points of salvation history; it also provides an opportunity for the preacher to speak of God's choice of the elect and the "rush of the Spirit" that will be sacramentally actualized in chrismation at the Easter Vigil.

The responsorial psalm (23:1 – 3, 3 – 4, 5, 6), with its suggested refrain, "The Lord is my shepherd, there is nothing I shall want," narrates three actions of the shepherd and host that portray God's protective activity toward his elect: leading them to streams of water, anointing their heads with oil and spreading the table before them. Patristic tradition saw in these three references types of the baptismal washing, confirmational anointing and eucharistic banquet, a reinterpretation that meshes with the reinterpretation of the 1 Samuel reading already mentioned.

Ephesians 5:8 – 14 announces the light/darkness motif with a typical Pauline yoking of *logos* and *ethos:* one does not perform good deeds in order to save oneself, but because Christ has made us children of the light, "deeds of light" flow from our Christic transformation. John 9:1 – 41, the narrative of Jesus' encounter with the man born blind, provides numerous images for initiation preaching. Some preachers may want to focus simply on Jesus' self-identification as the light of the world, manifested in his use of matter (saliva, soil, water) to mediate his saving power. This provides a perfect opportunity to emphasize the "sacramental principle" at work in the texts and in the ceremonies of Christian initiation. Other preachers may discuss the social consequences of proclaiming belief in Jesus: Just as the man born blind is alienated from his neighbors, his acquaintances, the religious authorities and even his own parents because of his encounter with Jesus, so the elect may find themselves in tension with their former social circles as their behavior is increasingly directed by their faith. Still others may emphasize the final encounter between Jesus and the man born blind: Belief in ("seeing") Jesus as the Son of Man is only possible when Christ's grace removes blindness of heart; the scrutiny texts invoke this grace upon the elect.

Third Scrutiny The readings appointed for the Fifth Sunday of Lent in Year A (*Lectionary for Mass,* 34) ground the celebration of the third scrutiny. The water and light symbolism of the last two scrutinies climaxes in the life/death symbolism of this set of readings.

Ezekiel 37:12 – 14 presents the conclusion of the prophet's vision of the dry bones, a declaration that the restoration of Israel to its land will be like those in the grave being restored to life. The preacher might want to explore the individual and communal dimensions of risen life in Christ, life sustained by the spirit of God.

43

The responsorial psalm (130:1 – 2, 3 – 4, 5 – 6, 7 – 8), with its suggested refrain, "With the Lord there is mercy, and the fullness of redemption," highlights the task of the elect during this period of purification and enlightenment: to trust in the Lord's word and to wait upon his presence.

Romans 8:8 – 11 concentrates in almost blunt language on the central Christian hope: that the spirit of God who raised Jesus from the dead will dwell in us and raise our mortal bodies to life. Preachers could contrast resuscitation with resurrection, showing how God's spirit does not simply restore us to a past "golden age" but equips us to live by and in God's absolute future.

But towering over all these scriptural proclamations is John 11:1 – 45, the narrative of Jesus' raising of Lazarus; it is the high point of the Johannine "Book of Signs." One approach to preaching based on this gospel could focus on Jesus' liberation of Lazarus from earthly death: "Untie him and let him go free!" could become a refrain as the preacher addresses the various chains that bind himself, the faithful and the elect. Another approach would be to emphasize the contemporary implications of how the disciples are stretched out of their complacency by choosing to follow Jesus' lead: "Let us go along, to die with him."

I have found that the most powerful preaching on this gospel arises from imaginatively reconstructing Martha's journey of faith: her transformative journey is a progression from anger at an absent friend, to hope that the friend will still come through, to religious resignation in God's future promise, to the heart-breaking awareness that resurrection and life is already present in friendship with Jesus; the faith-journey of the elect should find echoes here.

Presentations Article 147 of the RCIA outlines the meaning and purpose of the ritual presentations of Creed and Lord's Prayer during the period of purification and enlightenment:

> With the catechumenal formation of the elect completed, the church lovingly entrusts to them the Creed and the Lord's Prayer . . . expressing the heart of the church's faith and prayer. These texts are presented in order to enlighten the elect. The Creed, as it recalls the wonderful deeds of God for the salvation of the human race, suffuses the vision of the elect with the sure light of faith. The Lord's Prayer fills them with a deeper realization of the new spirit of adoption by which they will call God their Father, especially in the midst of the eucharistic assembly.

Initiation preaching is a prized component of both events. As at the scrutinies, the RCIA prefers this preaching to be grounded in the scriptures proclaimed at the ceremony:

> After the readings and guided by them, the celebrant explains in the homily the meaning and importance of the Creed in relation to the teaching that the elect have already received and to the profession of faith that they must make at their baptism and uphold throughout their lives. (#159)
>
> After the gospel presentation, the celebrant in the homily explains the meaning and importance of the Lord's Prayer. (#181)

Presentation of the Creed The readings that have been appointed for the celebration of the Presentation of the Creed (*Lectionary for Mass,* 748) take precedence over the lenten weekday readings (RCIA, 158).

Deuteronomy 6:1 – 7 restates the same election/ command/promise dynamic that is found in the Genesis reading for the rite of acceptance into the order of catechumens. The conclusion of the reading is the first paragraph of the Jewish liturgical creed, the *Shema Israel,* traditionally recited twice daily. The preacher could show that a creed is not simply a declaration of beliefs but a self-implicating discourse; could recount stories (especially from the Holocaust) in which martyred Jews died with this text on their lips; or could demonstrate how a common creed forms a people and why the Christian creed is so important for Christian identity.

The responsorial psalm (19:8, 9, 10, 11), with its suggested refrain taken from John 6:68c, "Lord, you have the words of everlasting life," is an extended meditation on Torah, whose attributes and powers are lauded; the antiphon makes clear that for Christians, the word of God *par excellence* is found in the words (understood as including the deeds) of the Lord Jesus.

Two options are given for the New Testament letter: Romans 10:8 – 13, which presents conditions for salvation — "if you confess with your lips that Jesus is Lord and believe in your heart that God raised him from the dead" — that are especially important to evangelical Christians, and 1 Corinthians 15:1 – 8a or 1 – 4, both of which enshrine the Pauline *kerygma*. The preacher might explore with the elect the process by which Jesus preached the Reign of God and the church preached Jesus; in any case, the christological foundation of Christian belief is stressed in these readings.

Two options are also given for the gospel. If Matthew 16:13 – 18 is selected, it would be important to indicate that the crucial question posed by Jesus — "Who do you say I am?" — is in the plural and that Peter is not so much passing an individual quiz as declaring the disciples' (and, by implication, the church's) faith. The preacher can declare that the attempt to capture the meaning of Jesus as one of a string of dead heroes is faulty; the only adequate Christian confession of his meaning sees in him the ultimate manifestation of the living God and the fulfillment of that God's promises.

The dense affirmations found in John 12:44 – 50 are less vividly imaginative, but theologically richer, evocations of faith in Christ. In any event, John 3:16 ("God loved the world so much, he gave us his only Son, that all who believe in him might have eternal life"), the verse before the gospel, might provide a powerful conclusion to the preaching as well as provide a scriptural passage for the catechumens to memorize along with the church's composition of the creed.

Presentation of the Lord's Prayer   The readings appointed for the Presentation of the Lord's Prayer (*Lectionary for Mass,* 749) likewise substitute for the weekday lenten choices (RCIA, 179).

Hosea 11:1b, 3 – 4, 8c – 9 can be read as an extended meditation on what "Father" means in the Lord's Prayer and why Jesus characteristically referred to his God as "Abba." In an age and culture when the image of God as Father is under attack (due, I suspect, not only to anger at oppressive patriarchal structures but also to very personal difficulties between fathers and their children), the preacher might want to retrieve something of the biblical understanding of fatherhood applied to God while reminding his hearers that the ascription remains metaphorical ("I am God not man, the Holy One present among you").

Since the first option for the responsorial psalm has already been used with the same refrain at the second scrutiny, Year A, the preacher may want to explicate Psalm 103:1 – 2, 8 and 10, 11 – 12, 13 and 18, whose suggested refrain — "As a father is kind to his children, so kind is the Lord to those who fear him" — reinforces and enriches the presentation of God's fatherhood announced in the Hosea reading.

Two options are also provided for the New Testament letter. Romans 8:14 – 17, 26 – 27 reminds us that we can only pray the Lord's Prayer because faith and baptism make us adopted children of God and that prayer is ultimately the Spirit's wordless action within us, not simply the recitation of a fixed verbal formula. Galatians 4:4 – 7 also yokes the individual Christian's and the Christian community's ability to address God as "Abba" with our baptismal adoption.

Note that the gospel proclamation is done with special ceremony. The Matthean form of the text is used according to RCIA, 180, but *Lectionary for Mass*, 749, conflates the two scriptural versions of the Lord's Prayer. While such a conflation would be anathema to exegetes, I think prefacing the familiar Lord's Prayer text with the Lucan emphasis on the "Our Father" as a prayer that marks Christian fellowship is an important element for the presentation ceremony.

Preparation Rites on Holy Saturday The RCIA provides quite a variety of ceremonies to bring the period of purification and enlightenment to a close and to prepare the elect for the initiatory events of the Easter Vigil: the recitation of the Creed, an "ephphetha" rite and/or the choosing of a baptismal name. Preaching could mark any or all of these events:

> In proximate preparation for the celebration of the sacraments of initiation:
> 1. The elect are to be advised that on Holy Saturday they should refrain from their usual activities, spend their time in prayer and reflection and, as far as they can, observe a fast.
> 2. When it is possible to bring the elect together on Holy Saturday for reflection and prayer, some or all of the following rites may be celebrated as an immediate preparation for the sacraments: the presentation of the Lord's Prayer, if it has been deferred . . . , the "return" or recitation of the Creed . . . , the ephphetha rite . . . , the choosing of a baptismal name. (#185)

Where indicated in the particular rites, a brief homily or an explanation of the text follows the reading of the word of God. (#190)

Recitation of the Creed Article 194 of the RCIA provides only gospel readings for the ceremony of the recitation of the Creed, although it notes that "another appropriate reading may be chosen." Rather than a "complete" liturgy of the word—with Old Testament proclamation, responsorial psalm, New Testament letter and gospel — only a single gospel passage is proclaimed. Matthew 16:13 – 17 serves as the first gospel option for the presentation of the Creed; proclaiming and preaching this text when the elect recite the Creed could form a powerful *inclusio.* Alternatively, John 6:35, 63 – 71 poetically situates the spiritual condition of the elect facing Easter Vigil baptism: unlike the crowds of the gospel story, they, with the disciples, have cast their lot with Jesus; they have learned to feed on his word as the bread of life. The preacher might remind them that on this very evening they will be feeding on the eucharistic bread of life to whose banquet their faith has led them.

Ephphetha Rite *Lectionary for Mass,* 750, provides the single gospel reading assigned to the ephphetha rite: Mark 7:31 – 37. No alternatives are suggested. Once again, the preacher could emphasize the "sacramental principle" at work in the gospel narrative: Just as Jesus uses material things (touch, saliva, gazing at the sky, groaning and verbal command) to accomplish his saving work, so the church uses material things as signs and instruments ("sacraments") of Jesus' ongoing salvific encounters. Personally, I am fascinated by the Marcan detail that Jesus "emitted a groan": whether this symbolically represents Jesus taking upon himself the wounded condition of humanity or depicts his anger and grief over the brokenness of the world as he battles death-dealing forces, it clearly presents a Jesus who is on the side of human liberation.

Choosing of a Baptismal Name Finally, RCIA, 201, provides a non-exhaustive list of five pericopes, one of which should be proclaimed during the ceremony of choosing a baptismal name. Once again, a complete liturgy of the word is not prescribed. Genesis 17:1 – 7 again presents the election/command/promise dynamic in its retelling of the foundation of the Abrahamic covenant; here the focus would be on the change of name from *Abram* ("exalted ancestor") to *Abraham* ("ancestor of a multitude"), a change indicating complete assurance in the covenant promises. A similar set of name changes appears in Isaiah 62:1–5 but is now applied to the entire people, whose status shifts from exiles and outcasts to citizens and spouses. Revelation 3:11–13, a portion of the letter to the angel of the church of Philadelphia, is quite mysterious: Christ promises to sign those who are faithful to him with the name of his God, the name of the new Jerusalem and his own name. Preaching on these three names might employ the notion of "signed, sealed and delivered." Matthew 16:13–18 once again repeats Peter's confession of faith that has marked the presentation and return of the Creed, but John 1:40–42 places the change of Simon's name to *Cephas* in a different context, stressing the new creation that one becomes by becoming a disciple of Jesus.

Celebration of the Sacraments of Initiation

Article 206 of the RCIA clarifies the meaning of the final step in the Christian initiation of adults:

> The third step in the Christian initiation of adults is the celebration of the sacraments of baptism, confirmation and eucharist. Through this final step the elect, receiving pardon for their sins, are admitted into the people of God. They are graced with adoption as children of God and are led by the Holy Spirit into the promised fullness of time begun in Christ and, as they share in the eucharistic sacrifice and meal, even to a foretaste of the kingdom of God.

Later articles sketch the preaching focus for this event:

> The usual time for the celebration of the sacraments of initiation is the Easter Vigil . . . , at which preferably the bishop

himself presides as celebrant. . . . As indicated in the Roman Missal, "Easter Vigil" . . . , the conferral of the sacraments follows the blessing of the water. (#207)

When the celebration takes place outside the usual time . . . care should be taken to ensure that it has a markedly paschal character. . . . Thus the texts for one of the ritual Masses "Christian Initiation: Baptism" given in the Roman Missal are used, and the readings are chosen from those given in the Lectionary for Mass, "Celebration of the Sacraments of Initiation apart from the Easter Vigil." (#208)

Commenting on the seven possible Old Testament readings, their accompanying responsorial psalms and the epistle and its psalm that are appointed for the vigil (as well as commenting on the texts in *Lectionary for Mass,* 752 – 756: nine readings from the Old Testament, eleven responsorial psalms, thirteen non-gospel New Testament readings, seven verses before the gospel and twelve gospel pericopes) is impossible in a monograph of this size. Besides, I contend that the Vigil is best celebrated as an extended night-watch rather than an expanded liturgy of the word. Perhaps after the opening light service after sunset, a reading with psalm and collect could be proclaimed every hour (or every half-hour). Various preachers (ordained and unordained) might offer a few reflections on the reading/psalm/collect as they are celebrated, but the major response to the proclamation unit would be extended meditative silence. Then either in the dead of night or just before dawn, the epistle and gospel could be proclaimed with the Easter homily following, leading the community into the baptismal, chrismal and eucharistic rites.

Scripture scholars assert that the traditions concerning Jesus' resurrection have taken literary form in three major formats. The earliest seem to be short declarative sentences embedded in the *kerygma* and frequently express a contrast: Jesus, whom humanity rejected and killed, God has vindicated and raised up. A second genre consists of empty-tomb stories; but finding no body in Jesus' tomb does not automatically lead to faith in his resurrection because the absence of the body can be explained in a variety of ways. The third literary pattern comprises appearance narratives in which the risen Lord encounters individuals and groups; here the sacred authors strain at the edge of language to recount something literally unimaginable — affirming that the Risen One is the very Jesus whom they had known and witnessed die but who now lives a human existence beyond the confines of space, time and death. Preaching at the Easter Vigil should respect these scriptural categories rather than painting an "eyewitness account" of Jesus' exit from the tomb with Hollywood-style special effects.

Matthew 28:1 – 10, the gospel appointed for the Vigil in Year A, combines an empty tomb narrative with an appearance story. While the preacher might be tempted to embellish the "apocalyptic stage props" employed by the sacred author (earthquake, angel dressed in dazzling garments appearing like lightning, guards paralyzed like dead men), I believe a more authentic focus would be on the Christian *kerygma* proclaimed by the angel and on the missionary implications of believing the angel's message. The preacher might also note the social status of the women who receive the angelic proclamation, the vision of the risen Lord and the commission to evangelize the other disciples.

The empty-tomb story appointed for the Easter Vigil in Year B, Mark 16:1 – 8, presents a conundrum: If, as many scripture scholars think, this represents the original ending of Mark, how could the Easter message ever have been proclaimed if the women "said nothing to anyone"? The preacher could emphasize the typically Marcan stress on Jesus as the Crucified One who "goes before" the disciples on the journey that is destined for him by God.

Luke 24:1 – 12 also recounts an empty-tomb story, but here the women communicate what they have experienced at the tomb to the disciples. The preacher could stress the Lucan theme of women among the followers of Jesus (this gospel has the most individual women named as well as a reference to "the other women with them") or the geographical progress of Luke – Acts (here the men in dazzling garments remind them of what Jesus said in Galilee, not that he will meet them there, because Jesus' whole ministry had already reached its fulfillment in Jerusalem and the Christian message will go forth from Jerusalem to the ends of the earth). The preacher could also stress the divided reception of the women's message by the apostles, impelling Peter to visit the tomb (a frank recognition of the varying degrees of resurrection faith within the Christian community). The question posed to the women could serve as keynote, refrain and conclusion for Easter Vigil preaching: "Why do you search for the Living One among the dead? He is not here; he has been raised up!"

Period of Postbaptismal Catechesis or Mystagogy

The length and purpose of the final period of the RCIA, the period of postbaptismal catechesis, is sketched in article 7.4:

> The final period extends through the whole Easter season and is devoted to the postbaptismal catechesis or mystagogy. It is a time for deepening the Christian experience, for spiritual growth and for entering more fully into the life and unity of the community.

Further articles clarify the preaching focus of the season:

> This is a time for the community and the neophytes together to grow in deepening their grasp of the paschal mystery and in making it a part of their lives through meditation on the gospel, sharing in the eucharist and doing the works of charity. (#244)

53

Since the distinctive spirit and power of the period of post-baptismal catechesis or mystagogy derive from the new, personal experience of the sacraments and of the community, its main setting is the so-called Masses for neophytes, that is, the Sunday Masses of the Easter season. Besides being occasions for the newly baptized to gather with the community and share in the mysteries, these celebrations include particularly suitable readings from the lectionary, especially the readings for Year A. (#247)

The homily and, as circumstances suggest, the general intercessions should take into account the presence and needs of the neophytes. (#248)

Although RCIA, 247, indicates that the Eastertide Sunday readings of Year A are especially suitable for mystagogy, the *Lectionary for Mass* (unlike its directives concerning the scrutiny Masses in Lent) does not indicate that they can be substituted for the readings that have appointed in the other cycles when neophytes are present. The revised "Introduction" to the *Lectionary for Mass,* 100, outlines the unique organization of the Sunday Eastertide readings:

The gospel readings for the first three Sundays recount the appearances of the risen Christ. The readings about the Good Shepherd are assigned to the Fourth Sunday. On the Fifth, Sixth and Seventh Sundays, there are excerpts from the Lord's discourse and prayer at the last supper.

The first reading is from Acts, in a three-year cycle of parallel and progressive selections: material is presented on the life of the primitive church, its witness and its growth.

For the reading from the apostles, 1 Peter is in Year A, 1 John in Year B, Revelation in Year C. These are the texts that seem to fit in especially well with the spirit of joyous faith and sure hope proper to this season.

Because the preaching focus for the Eastertide mystagogical period is on consolidating sacramental experience and empowering for mission, preaching during this period might take the form of a "sermon series" based on one of these sets of readings.

Preaching the Easter Gospel Readings If the preacher chooses to preach a series based on the gospel readings, Eastertide will be marked by three distinct periods. After the empty-tomb stories of the Vigil gospels, various appearance narratives mark the Second and Third Sundays of Easter.

John 20:19–31 is the gospel appointed for the Second Sunday of Easter in all three Sunday cycles; the preacher could explicate how the resurrection transforms the disciples from fearful to fearless human beings; discourse on how the risen Lord empowers the disciples through gifts (peace, Holy Spirit), missions (sent as the Father sent Jesus, forgiving people's sins) and gestures (showing hands and side, breathing upon them); present Thomas's confession of faith as the pinnacle of human insight into Jesus; or apply the risen Lord's beatitude concerning those who have not seen and yet believed to the neophytes and the faithful.

The Third Sunday of Easter continues the appearance narratives. In Year A preaching on the Emmaus story in Luke 24:13–35 might parallel the four movements of the Christian eucharistic liturgy (assembly, scripture proclamation and response, table fellowship, missioning) with the interchanges of Cleopas and his companion with Jesus. The gospel appointed for the Third Sunday of Easter in Year B, Luke 24:35–48, also contains these four movements but in a different order (assembly, meal, scripture proclamation and response, mission), which could relate less to the eucharistic assembly and more to the domestic and household worship of Christians (and could also provide a justification for scheduling an *agape*-meal for the neophytes and faithful to share). In Year C the appearance narratives in John 21:1–19 could inspire the preacher to point out how one cannot return to business as usual once the power of the resurrection has seized one; the poignant story of Peter's rehabilitation (the one who denied his friend three times now professing his love for his Lord three times) could remind neophytes and faithful alike that Christian leadership and service does not require perfect human beings but those with generous and loving hearts.

Good Shepherd Sunday has gospel passages taken from John 10 in all three cycles; at present this Sunday has been designated as World Day of Prayer for Vocations and offers the preacher an opportunity to challenge the neophytes to consider how their baptismal commitment will be lived out: in vocations to matrimony, to dedicated lay service to church and/or world, to vowed life, or to ordination to the diaconate or presbyterate.

Various discourses from the Johannine account of the Last Supper mark the Fifth and Sixth Sundays of Eastertide in all cycles, and the great "high priestly" prayer of John 17 appears on the Seventh Sunday of Easter. Themes of following Jesus as way, truth and life, abiding in him, mutual love for members of the Christian community, fervent prayer for "another Paraclete" (the Spirit) and Christian unity all cry out for mystagogical treatment.

The entire series finds its climax in the Pentecost gospels, where the rivers of living water flowing from within Jesus (Vigil) and the gift of the Holy Spirit (Day) impel all who have been baptized, neophytes and faithful alike, to carry on the reconciling mission of Jesus in the world.

Preaching the Acts of the Apostles Alternatively, the preacher could create an Eastertide series by explicating the Acts of the Apostles. Idealized portraits of the primitive Christian community occur in all cycles on the Second Sunday of Easter; the preacher might want to show how *kerygma* (proclamation), *didache* (teaching), *koinonia* (communal life), *diakonia* (service) and *leitourgia* (worship) mark every authentic Christian community from the days of the apostles until now. The Second and Third Sundays of Easter rehearse the foundational preaching of the apostles (especially Peter's Pentecost speech) and the conflict it creates. The remaining Sundays of Eastertide disclose the church's ministry *ad intra* (the designation of the Seven, the Council of Jerusalem, the election of Matthias) and *ad extra* (Peter's baptism of Cornelius and his household, Philip's preaching in Samaria, Paul and Barnabas founding churches in various locations). It should be easy for the preacher to indicate how the local community continues these missions in contemporary practice.

Preaching the Second Readings A third alternative would be for the preacher to construct a sermon series for Eastertide based on the New Testament non-gospel reading. The use of 1 Peter in Year A would have the clearest connection with mystagogical preaching, since some scripture scholars have considered the treatise a baptismal liturgy or homily. In Year B, 1 John is read and its emphases on community life, keeping Christ's commandments and love for one another in word and deed are salutary reminders to neophytes and faithful: "See what love the Father has bestowed on us in letting us be called children of God! Yet that is what we are" (1 John 3:1; Fourth Sunday of Easter, Year B). Most problematic would be a series based on the Revelation pericopes in Year C, yet the presence of "the First and the Last and the One who lives" pervades the exotic imagery and visionary exuberance of these texts.

Preaching the Liturgy Finally, the preacher might want to offer a eucharistic mystagogy during Eastertide, preaching on the depth meanings of the various rites and ceremonies that the neophytes now share with the faithful. Exploring the richness of the Eastertide prefaces is especially appealing to me, fleshing out the poetic declarations of the church's faith in the risen Christ:

He is the true Lamb who took away the sins of the world.
By dying he destroyed our death;
by rising he restored our life. (Easter I)

He has made us children of the light,
rising to new and everlasting life.
He has opened the gates of heaven
to receive his faithful people.
His death is our ransom from death;
his resurrection is our rising to life. (Easter II)

In him a new age has dawned,
the long reign of sin is ended,
a broken world has been renewed,
and [hu]man[kind] is once again made whole. (Easter IV)

Having summarized the expectations presented to the preacher by the RCIA, we will focus in the next chapter on the process of preparing to preach.

Chapter 3

Preparing Liturgical Preaching for the Rites of Christian Initiation

■

Having defined liturgical preaching in general and having explored the types of liturgical preaching called for by the RCIA, we now turn to the process by which this preaching might be prepared.

I do not intend to offer a recipe for "fail-safe" homilies, as though one could mix three cups of scriptural quotations, two tablespoons of humorous or heartwarming illustrations, a dash of the liturgical season and a *soupçon* of poetry to produce a sermonic *pièce-de-résistance*. While it is helpful to have a checklist of elements from which the preacher may make choices in preparing preaching, I do not believe that combining these elements in certain fixed proportions guarantees a successful homily.

Nor am I interested in prescribing a regimen for preparing preaching for the weekend eucharist: "Read over the scriptural and liturgical texts on the Sunday before you are scheduled to preach. Do exegesis of and

59

read commentaries about the gospel on Monday, the Hebrew scriptures (first reading *and* responsorial psalm) on Tuesday, the New Testament letter on Wednesday. Read *Time, U.S. News and World Report, The National Catholic Reporter, The Wanderer* and your diocesan newspaper on Thursday. Take Friday off. Write the homily on Saturday morning." While it is perhaps necessary to have fixed times and regular procedures for homily preparation, the demands of pastoral care make such a rigid schedule untenable.

What I offer instead is a checklist of ten activities that I have found helpful to engage in as I prepare to preach. Rarely will I spend equal amounts of time on all ten. I may even skip one or two of the activities as I prepare for a particular preaching occasion. But I know that my preaching suffers if I neglect any one of these activities for a length of time.

I presume that the preacher will pursue these ten activities in the context of prayer. As O. C. Edwards notes in a reflection on this process:

> There is no point in preaching if you do not believe in prayer. Preaching grows out of the conviction that life is about God, the God who was revealed in Jesus Christ and who is worshiped in the church. God's ordained servants . . . who lead his people in worship need to be persons of prayer themselves. And one of the things that all Christians should pray about is their work. While all of life should be an offering to God, the work one does is a matter of vocation, a matter of the particular task for which one was created and called. . . .
>
> Such prayer should not be confined to the beginning of the process, like the old custom of writing *J.M.J.* at the top of a page. Much of the working out of a sermon is an interior dialogue. In such a dialogue you can address God as easily as yourself. Doing so will change remarkably your attitude toward what you are doing.[1]

With that reminder of the spiritual context for preaching preparation, we now concentrate on a "Drafting Decalogue for Homily Development."

Position the Event

Irénée Henri Dalmais declares that "as an analysis of the term shows, the liturgy is an operation or action *(ergon);* it is not first and foremost a discourse *(logos)*."[2] It is not for nothing that the monastic Rule of St. Benedict refers to public worship as the *opus Dei* ("work of God") or that the *Old Gelasian Sacramentary* refers to the eucharistic prayer as the *canon actionis* (the "rule and norm of the liturgical action"). As an integral component of the liturgical event (rather than "time out" for the reading of the bulletin, guidance in ritual etiquette or entertainment at half-time), liturgical preaching has the character of proclamatory event. Liturgical preaching discloses the divine/human encounter transpiring in the midst of the worshiping assembly. Thus the preacher must be clear about what *event* the church is celebrating in a given liturgy — what *action* God and humanity contract. Clarity in the preacher's mind about the event celebrated should lead to clarity about the preacher's task.

In the Liturgical Cycle   Most initiation preaching will involve the intersection of the cycle of the liturgical year with rites proper to the initiation sequence itself. The reflections offered in chapter two are intended to help the preacher position the initiation rituals within the liturgical cycle. The liturgical cycle engages the church whether or not there are people to be initiated; the initiation cycle occurs only when people present themselves for full membership in the church.

Tensions between the two cycles can occur when those to be initiated are not present at all the eucharists in a given weekend. For example, on the Third, Fourth and Fifth Sundays of Lent the preacher might be tempted to use the great Johannine pericopes that are yoked to the scrutinies during Years B and C, even when there are no initiates present at a particular eucharist (I suspect to avoid having to prepare different homilies). Although it means extra work for the preacher and the liturgy planning team, in this circumstance two different sets of readings, homily, music choices, etc., are called for because the liturgical event being celebrated is different.

In the Lives of the Participants The preacher likewise should clarify how these rites encounter the human life-journeys of the initiates. Initiation rites will have quite different resonances for a baptized Lutheran who is becoming Roman Catholic after fifty years in a mixed marriage, a Pentecostal not baptized in water who is changing denominations after ten years as a storefront holiness preacher, a baptized but uncatechized adult who has discovered Christian faith in the midst of a struggle with chemical addiction, and an unbaptized ten-year-old whose previously alienated Catholic parents never presented her for baptism. Some preachers will be tempted to produce "one-size-fits-all" initiation homilies that could be filed for future use. While it is helpful for a preacher to maintain a file of past preaching (mostly so that the same themes, approaches and examples will not be repeated from year to year), each preaching event demands grappling with how God is interacting with this unique portion of humanity in light of the scripture and the liturgy. Generic homilies do not and cannot.

In the History of the Worshiping Assembly Every parish has its own history: the "pillars of the church," the "secret saints," the founding pastor and his beleaguered associates, etc. Recalling this history concretizes the way in which God journeys with the local congregation. At one Easter Vigil at which I presided, the lector choked up and emotionally broke down as he was proclaiming the story of the binding of Isaac. A baby girl had just been born to him and his wife, and the notion of sacrificing one's first-born hit him with overwhelming force as he proclaimed the scriptures. Not only was

I able to preach at that Vigil how the word of God encounters us with unexpected force, but I could refer to the experience the next year with nods of recognition from the assembly.

The preacher must also clarify, however, that initiates are not simply being welcomed to a local congregation but are joining a global church. The history of the local worshiping assembly must be placed in the context of the "cloud of witnesses" who have handed on Christian faith to the present day and the multitudes to come who will "await with joyful hope the coming of our Savior, Jesus Christ." Especially in the United States, where congregationalist notions of churches as voluntary organizations is strong, emphasis on the universal dimension of Christian communion is needed.

In Its Cultural Context The preacher should be sensitive to the social and political issues contextualizing a given act of worship. If the nation mobilizes its military, if the town suffers a natural disaster, if the major employer for the parishioners announces a plant closing, these events must be addressed even if they do not easily mesh with the liturgical cycle. Ignoring the cultural context runs the risk of denying the presence of God at work in history, of consigning God's action to past ages and suggesting that God has abandoned us now. Investigating the tradition can help the preacher locate where God is acting in the present, by learning how other faith-filled people identified God's action in the past.

Investigate the Tradition

Historical research has made it clear that patterns of Christian initiation vary greatly over both time as well as geography.[3] Investigating the traditions of Christian initiation can provide some help in clarifying what is essential

63

and normative in a given ritual and what is only peripheral. Knowing in which era a given text or practice arose and also understanding how it functioned in its original cultural context may illuminate its present use. This investigation should free the preacher to make pastoral applications and adaptations that are respectful of Christian heritage yet will also be responsive to contemporary concerns.

Jewish Structures of Initiation Because Jesus was a Jew and his earliest followers were Jews, knowledge of Jewish initiation practices sheds light on Christian initiation. The *berit milah* ("covenant of circumcision") ceremony, also known as a *bris,* parallels and contrasts with baptism. The fundamental actions are quite diverse: the removal of the foreskin (symbolically marking the organ of generation as the means by which the Abrahamic covenant is continued and fulfilled) vs. immersion or washing with water (symbolically killing/saving or cleansing as the means by which one enters the Christic covenant). The personnel involved are likewise diverse: a *mohel* (ritual circumciser) and *sandok* (honoree who holds the infant for circumcision) in addition to parents, family and friends (the father's role is especially prominent) vs. ordained minister (priest or deacon), sponsors and godparents in addition to parents, family and friends. It is not too overreaching to say that this form of Jewish initiation is fundamentally a domestic ritual emphasizing the male infant's familial and ethnic ties, while Christian baptism emphasizes entry into a social structure that supersedes family and ethnic heritage.

The preacher also should be aware of initiation patterns in which adults of Gentile heritage become Jews. These patterns traditionally involve ritual questioning, circumcision (in the case of a male) and bathing. Once again, comparisons and contrasts with Christian initiation patterns can be drawn.

New Testament Patterns   Knowledge of Jewish initiation patterns should make the New Testament foundation for Christian initiation more intelligible. The baptism of repentance preached and performed by John at the Jordan River does not provide an exact parallel to Christian initiation, yet it does highlight the eschatological urgency of baptism. Its relation to general Jewish lustrations, Essene purificatory water rituals and prophetic symbolic action remains, however, disputed among scholars. Jesus' own baptism by John provides the grounding for such theologies of Christian initiation as pneumatic anointing, divine adoption or designation for mission.

Various perspectives on baptism appear in the Pauline letters and First Peter. The Acts of the Apostles makes it clear that there is no single ritual pattern of Christian initiation that can claim normative status. These New Testament texts, in all their variety, do witness to a three-fold overriding conviction: that in Christ God has offered humanity an alternative to the life of sin, that the Spirit empowers human beings to accept God's offer, and that accepting God's offer of salvation involves incorporation in the community of salvation. Present-day initiation preaching proclaims this New Testament conviction in terms intelligible and credible for contemporary auditors.

Patristic Patterns   Ancient Christian writers from the *Didache* through Gregory the Great demonstrate how the reality of new life in Christ, mediated through Christian initiation, took form in text and ceremony in the cultures around the Mediterranean basin. While it is highly unlikely that any initiates in the United States will be invited to stand barefoot on goatskin (symbolically trampling underfoot the garments that covered the first humans after the Fall), spit toward the west (symbolically rejecting Satan who dwells in darkness) or have their heads wrapped up in turbans (symbolically signifying membership in the "royal priesthood" after water baptism), knowledge of these ancient practices can assist the preacher in making connections between Christian initiation and contemporary cultural conventions. Chapter four explores this patristic heritage in some detail.

Medieval Patterns   About the year 811 CE, Charlemagne sent a questionnaire to all the archbishops of his empire inquiring what they did in initiating Christians and what they taught that the various ceremonies meant. The responses sent to the "most Christian emperor" bear witness to changes in the ritual structuring of water baptism, chrismation and eucharist as the climactic elements in Christian initiation as well as changes in its theology. The medieval period also produced a wealth of commentaries on the Lord's Prayer (a frequent theme was the yoking of its seven petitions with other "sacred sevens," e.g., the gifts of the Holy Spirit and the beatitudes) and on the Creed.

The high Middle Ages produced a remarkable systematic sacramental theology in which questions of matter and form, minister and recipient, sacramental character and efficacy were all addressed. Many of the scholastic theologians presented the sacraments as divinely instituted remedies for sin. In this period the custom arose of paralleling the components of the sacramental system with the stages of human growth, a custom with far-reaching consequences for the later theology of the sacraments of initiation.

Reformation and Counter-Reformation Patterns
The reconfiguring of Western Christianity as a result of the sixteenth-century Reformation had profound effects on Christian initiation. Roman Catholicism (in contrast with Orthodoxy, which maintained the unity of water baptism, chrismation and eucharist whenever initiation was celebrated, either during infancy or adulthood) continued a medieval pattern in which most members were

water baptized in infancy and then confirmed and eucharistized (in that order) in childhood. The "mainstream" Reformers continued to practice infant baptism, denied the sacramental status of confirmation and began the practice of examining young people's intellectual grasp of the fundamentals of Christian teaching before admitting them to eucharist. The Radical Reformers denied the sacramental status of infant baptism, asserting that "believers' baptism" is the pattern enshrined in the New Testament. Membership in the Christian church became affiliation with a particular denomination. In spite of much bi- and multi-denominational theological discussion and landmark documents such as the World Council of Churches' *Baptism, Eucharist and Ministry,* the positions that were taken by Western Christians in the sixteenth century continue to frame practice and theory for many contemporary congregations.

Investigating the tradition as I have sketched it here involves more than simply accumulating historical data. One does not engage these records out of antiquarian interest or to canonize one era as a golden age of Christian initiation against which all others should be judged. Rather, the preacher studies the biblical and historical documentation concerning Christian initiation to make informed decisions about present directions in initiation preaching: what approaches lead to theological and pastoral gridlock, what texts unsurpassably connect us with our heritage, what ceremonies authentically enact the sacramental mystery?

Identify the Resources

There are many resources available to assist the preacher in investigating the biblical and historical traditions concerning Christian initiation and the present form of its rites. I would recommend the following publications as trustworthy guides.

67

Scripture Translations and Commentaries

There is no substitute for engaging the scriptural texts by reading and pondering them in their original languages. Many contemporary Roman Catholic preachers, however, are not fluent in Hebrew, Aramaic and Greek, even if they may have studied these languages in their ministerial formation programs. And the press of pastoral duties might keep them from immersing themselves in the original texts anyway. Preachers should, therefore, have and regularly consult a variety of vernacular translations. For English translations, I recommend the *New American Bible,* the *New English Bible,* the *New Jerusalem Bible,* and the *New Revised Standard Version* (avoid paraphrases such as the *Good News Bible*).

The preacher also needs a personal library of instruments for more deeply engaging the scriptural texts: concordances for the various translations, gospel parallels, "dictionaries" of biblical theology (ranging in complexity from John L. McKenzie's one-volume *Dictionary of the Bible* to the five-volume [with supplement] *Interpreter's Dictionary of the Bible* and the multivolume German series in translation, *Theological Dictionary of the Old / New Testament).*

In addition, a preacher should develop a library of commentaries on the individual books of scripture. One-volume commentaries covering the entire Bible include the primarily British *New Catholic Commentary on Sacred Scripture* and the primarily American *New Jerome Biblical Commentary.* Multivolume commentaries range in depth and complexity from William Barclay's *Daily Bible Study* series (filled with folksy illustrations appropriate to an earlier generation in the United Kingdom but to be used with caution by Roman Catholics because of some of Barclay's theological presuppositions) to the *Message of the Old/New Testament* series (published by Michael Glazier/ Liturgical Press) and the specialist commentaries in the *Anchor Bible* and *Hermeneia* series.

Liturgical Commentaries Just as there is no substitute for reading the biblical text, so there is no substitute for reading the foundational liturgical documents. To confirm that one's preaching reflects the church's desires, one should frequently return to the *Constitution on the Sacred Liturgy,* the *General Instruction of the Roman Missal,* the *Introduction to the Lectionary for Mass* and the *praenotanda* to the *Rite of Christian Initiation of Adults.*

Like the scriptural commentaries mentioned above, there are a variety of liturgical commentaries that interpret the readings, presidential texts, songs and ceremonies prescribed for the reformed Roman Rite. They range in size and complexity from the one-volume seasonal commentaries of Kevin Irwin (those titled *Lent* and *Easter* would be especially helpful for initiation preaching) to the four-volume commentary by Adrian Nocent named *The Liturgical Year* and to the multivolume *Days of the Lord* series.

Subscription Series The workaholic pastor whom I worked with and mentioned in chapter one never, to my knowledge, opened a scriptural or liturgical commentary in preparing his preaching. Instead, he subscribed to five "homily services" that provided complete sermons for a given set of readings. For him, homily preparation consisted of reading all five services and stitching together paragraphs from each until he reached a twenty-five minute talk. While the insights were usually respectable and the prose style acceptable, I am not sure the parish ever heard a genuine homily from his lips. As *Fulfilled in Your Hearing* (FIYH) accurately asserts:

> [The] pastoral dimension of the homily is the principal reason why some homily services, especially those that do little more than provide ready-to-preach homilies, can actually be a hindrance to effective preaching. Since the homily is integrally related to the liturgy, and since the liturgy presupposes a community that gathers to celebrate it, the homily is by definition related to a community. Homily services can be helpful in the

interpretation of scriptural texts (though generally not as much as some basic exegetical resources) and give some ideas on how these texts can be related to contemporary human concerns. But they cannot provide individual preachers with specific indications of how these texts can be heard by the particular congregations to whom they will preach. (#58)

Because there are so many homily services on the market, I will not attempt to evaluate them here. The most useful aids do not provide canned texts that the preacher can read word-for-word to the congregation, or even homily outlines with appropriate illustrations and points to emphasize, but "idea starters" — questions to pose to the scriptural texts, rites and ceremonies from other traditions celebrating the same liturgical event; quotations from poetry, plays and novels illustrative of the celebration's focus; or news items that have a claim on the congregation's life of discipleship. If the preacher's budget forces a choice between investing in the scriptural and liturgical commentaries described above and subscribing to a homily service, I would recommend the former. The journal *Catechumenate,* while not strictly a homily service, provides excellent reflections on the Lord's Day scriptures from an initiation perspective in the ongoing "Sunday Word" column.

Analyze the Auditors

Because a homily is not simply a message but a message *from* Someone *to* some people *through* someone, understanding the condition of those who will receive the message is terribly important. As O. C. Edwards notes:

> Really to engage in preaching . . . means that we say something that we consider important to particular people . . . and we say it in such a way that they can understand it, will be interested in it, and, we pray, be persuaded by it. For that to happen, we must know to whom we are speaking.[4]

Analyzing the auditors at an initiation liturgy reveals just how complex the preaching situation is.

Catechumens In the terminology of the RCIA, catechumens are distinguished from inquirers, also called sympathizers (the proper subjects of the precatechumenate), and the elect (those committed to final preparation before baptism). As the National Statutes for the Catechumenate approved by the National Conference of Catholic Bishops in 1986 reminds us:

> The term "catechumen" should be strictly reserved for the unbaptized who have been admitted into the order of catechumens; the term "convert" should be reserved strictly for those converted from unbelief to Christian belief and never used of those baptized Christians who are received into the full communion of the Catholic Church. (#2)

By careful analysis of New Testament conversionary preaching, scripture scholars have extracted what they consider the core of Christian witness, which they have termed the *kerygma* (proclamation). C. H. Dodd summarizes its primitive Pauline form as follows:

> The prophecies are fulfilled, and the new Age is inaugurated by the coming of Christ.
> He was born of the seed of David.
> He died according to the Scriptures, to deliver us out of the present evil age.
> He was buried.
> He rose on the third day according to the Scriptures.
> He is exalted at the right hand of God, as Son of God and Lord of quick and dead.
> He will come again as Judge and Savior of all.[5]

Notice that the kerygma is almost entirely a series of statements about Jesus: He comes from Jewish heritage; he fulfills Jewish expectations; his death, resurrection and exaltation manifest God's will toward humankind; he bears ultimate significance for the destiny of humanity. While one could spend much energy unpacking the assumptions behind these statements (e.g., that God exists, that God intervenes in human history) and the thought-world in which they are formulated (e.g., how one man's death could redeem humanity), these lapidary phrases continue to present what is distinctive about Christian belief.

If we take catechumens seriously as auditors of our preaching, then every homily at which they are present must have a kerygmatic component and every sermon must proclaim Jesus crucified, risen and exalted as the decisive reality for authentic human living. Catechists can inform the preacher about particular issues that have arisen as the catechumens explore the Christian message and its implications for their lives; this, in turn, can become a springboard for preaching.

I sometimes wonder if it would be possible to preach directly from catechumens' questions. The rhetorical patterns of much patristic initiation preaching strikes me as directly addressing the questions of the auditors.

Candidates for Full Communion Candidates for full communion hear initiation preaching differently than catechumens do. They have already been claimed by and for Christ in baptism. Many have already heard and have committed themselves to the way of Christ. The issue for candidates is denominational affiliation, discovering which tradition most adequately enshrines (or least fiercely deforms) the life of the gospel. The 1986 National Statutes state:

> Those who have already been baptized in another church or ecclesial community should not be treated as catechumens or so designated. Their doctrinal and spiritual preparation for reception into full Catholic communion should be determined according to the individual case, that is, it should depend on the extent to which the baptized person has led a Christian life within a community of faith and been appropriately catechized to deepen his or her inner adherence to the church. (#30)

Preaching to catechumens and candidates together is complicated because so much of Catholic church life is mediated either through technical vocabulary rarely used in non-church contexts or in terms that have quite different resonances than in the wider culture. The more the preacher can help catechumens and candidates grasp the interlocking nature of Catholic belief and practice, the better.

The Elect Preaching to the elect will take a different tone than preaching to catechumens, becoming less the disclosure of Catholic doctrine and behavior and more a declaration of what God is doing in their spiritual lives. Fortunately the rite of election, the scrutinies and the presentations all provide inexhaustible sources for homiletic reflection on the triumph of Christ's power over sin and death and the means by which Catholics appropriate and hand on this victory.

Sponsors and Godparents Sponsors and godparents frequently are neglected in initiation preaching. Addressing the initiates and the assembly as a whole can be so overwhelming that sponsors and godparents get short shrift in the homily. On occasion it may be appropriate for the preacher to highlight their roles as delegates of the assembly, as role models and faith companions for the catechumens and candidates, and as people on their own spiritual journeys.

Family and Friends Family and friends of the catechumens/elect and candidates also should be acknowledged occasionally in initiation preaching. Easiest for the preacher is the situation in which family and friends serve as the matrix from which the catechumens' and candidates' faith journeys begin and in which they will be lived out; this is frequently the case when the catechumen or candidate is the only non-Catholic in the household. More delicate would be the situation where family and friends are only peripherally committed or represent a smorgasbord of religious alliances. Most difficult are those situations in which family and friends actively oppose affiliation with Roman Catholicism. In this case, if family and friends are even present at the liturgical ceremonies, the preacher might acknowledge the sense of betrayal that family and friends might feel as a candidate embraces another religious heritage. Without compromising the truth claims of Roman Catholic Christianity, the preacher can point out how cherished values of other religions also appear in Roman Catholicism, albeit in symbolic forms that may appear strange to the outsider.

Pastoral Staff Members of the pastoral staff involved with initiation ministry should, on occasion, be directly addressed in liturgical preaching. After the dismissal rite, catechists will be explicating with catechumens what they together have heard from the preacher. It is quite appropriate to point out how God distributes gifts among the baptized and does not limit them to the ordained. The preacher might also address how catechists grow in faith in the very process of sharing it.

The Assembly The rest of the worshiping assembly cannot be ignored in initiation preaching. Some of the faithful, while not publicly involved in initiation ministry, are quite supportive of it. They enthusiastically welcome those to be initiated at Sunday Mass and actively engage in prayer for them. Another group is neutral. They can't understand why all this fuss is being made about those becoming Roman Catholic, but they will pray for them and even pay attention to preaching addressed to initiates as long as the preacher also addresses their religious concerns. Sad to say, there is also a group hostile to the initiation ceremonies, annoyed at the time added to the Sunday eucharist when the rites are performed with loving attention. Preachers need to care for all three groups of the faithful. The preacher will have a tendency to write off the third group as obstreperous and obtuse; while they are not the norm, the candidates need to experience the church "warts and all" if they are not to be fiercely disappointed with church membership after their mystagogy.

Diagnose the Preacher

In addition to analyzing the auditors, the preacher should engage in periodic self-examination, not only because such reflection is a fundamental condition for growth in the spiritual life but because such self-knowledge will disclose the particular biases brought by the preacher to the task.

Gender Because present Roman Catholic liturgical legislation restricts the liturgical homily to ordained (therefore male) ministers, there is a danger that characteristically female perspectives on the realities of faith may not be addressed in preaching. Male preachers need to discover the extent to which North American culture has formed their values (frequently prizing individual achievement, unbridled competition and suppression of strong emotions) and shaped their imaginations (frequently accenting a transcendent God who sovereignly establishes and powerfully enforces the moral order). Without identifying these influences, one may inadvertently overlook contrasting values and images upheld by the religious heritage.

Marital Status One's marital status also affects preaching. The unmarried frequently idealize or demonize spousal and family life, presenting trivial or wildly improbable illustrations in preaching. (There is a story told of the Irish grandmother remarking to her friend after a young priest preached on marriage: "I wish to

God I knew as little about marriage as that priest does!")
The married, however, may be less naturally attentive to
the singles, widows, separated and divorced in the congregation. In addition, the married need to beware lest
they present their own family life as a model to be emulated by all.

Personality Type In recent years the Myers–Briggs
Inventory (based on Jungian theories of personality) and
the Enneagram (based on Sufi mysticism) have become
popular tools for self-exploration among pastoral ministers. People even introduce themselves as an "INTJ" or a
"four with a five wing." Locating one's own personality
type can help a preacher identify the types of people
with whom one would most easily resonate as well as
those people whose stances would seem incomprehensi-
ble. I found that once I identified the characteristics of
my own personality I began to examine the content of
my preaching to make sure it would have something that
would appeal to other personality types.

Regularly assessing one's emotional stance before, during and after preaching is also helpful. When I was in
full-time parochial work some of my greatest stress
occurred when I preached at a funeral on Saturday morning, two weddings Saturday afternoon and the weekend
eucharist on Saturday evening; the shifts in tone of the
three liturgical events proved emotionally taxing. Because
the pulpit is neither the place for inappropriate personal
disclosure nor a disguised form of therapy, preachers must
understand and compensate for potentially disruptive
feelings when they are present.

Relation to Congregation One's status in the worshiping assembly strongly affects one's stance as a preacher.
Parish priests ("pastors") carry the weight of office in a
parish differently than parochial vicars ("assistants") do,
no matter how collaborative they may be in leadership

style. A non-parochial presbyter with a regular weekend preaching assignment in a particular community has a different link with that community than does a member of the "dawn patrol" facing a different congregation every weekend. Visiting preachers (frequently members of religious orders and/or missionaries) engage the assembly in still other ways. Deacons working in a parish as part of a pastoral internship before they are ordained presbyters also have a different connection to the worshiping assembly than a permanent deacon assigned to that parish does.

Preachers who regularly preach for the same assembly face certain dangers. They can pull their punches in preaching lest they offend the major donors. More subtly, the fear of wounding fragile members of the community (such as those facing the aftermath of abortion or extramarital affairs) may keep them from addressing controversial topics. Feuds with and grudges against certain parishioners or groups can unleash a preacher's tongue in destructive rage. The struggle to find novel and interesting ways to present the gospel and its implications can sap one's creativity and energy.

Visiting preachers face different dangers. Because they have no grounding in a particular assembly, they may be tempted to prepare a generic eucharistic talk that could be used on any occasion: "Have homily, will travel." Or they may be tempted to blast an assembly with a stirring call for social action or political protest without taking on the responsibility to pick up the pieces. Worst of all, visiting preachers may refuse to preach at all, informing the community that since they are simply visitors they have no way of really knowing how God is working in the community's life.

Arndt L. Halvorson reminds us that authenticity is of prime importance in the character of any preacher:

> Preachers usually assume that everyone is interested, as they are, in the quality of the sermon. They assume that people

will respond to a good sermon, one which is biblical, interesting, witty perhaps, searching, relevant, well delivered.

This is true, but first parishioners want to assess the preacher as a person. They will go home from church and say, "We seem to have a good preacher," but that doesn't settle the matter. Inevitably they add some assessment of the personal characteristics of the preacher. They say, "The preacher seems to be nice," or "nervous," or "standoffish," or "doesn't look you in the eye." That is, the parishioners want to hear good sermons, but they want to hear them from a good pastor. So they wait for an answer to the question, "What is our preacher like?" before they permit the sermons to have any impact.[6]

Theological Convictions Finally, preachers need to identify and critically embrace their fundamental theological convictions. Though some might claim (like Sergeant Joe Friday on *Dragnet*) to present "just the facts" of Christian faith, inevitably their theological convictions will color the "facts" they choose to present and the emphases they choose to give them. Few preachers are professional theologians, but all preachers should have enough professional theological education to present the content of the religious faith in which they participate in the most appropriate language possible.

Walter Burghardt points to ignorance of contemporary theology as one of the four major problems (along with fear of sacred scripture, lack of awareness about liturgical prayer and lack of proper preparation) that "prevent today's homily from being better than yesterday's sermon":

> Theology is indispensable for the word because it is the church's ceaseless effort to understand the word. . . . The church's search for understanding did not grind to a halt when I took my last theology exam; nor is the meaning of God's word preserved immobile in a Vatican capsule. Our basic Christian words, the words we preach, must be constantly recaptured, rethought: God, Christ, and Spirit; sin and redemption; church and sacraments; just and love; death and resurrection. . . . But until the clergy can read theology with

understanding and a critical eye, liturgical homiletics will continue to be impoverished.[7]

It is not enough for the preacher to identify and assert theological convictions; one must critically assess them for adequacy and coherence.

Converse with Others This prescription challenges a common, prevailing image of homily preparation in which the lone preacher retires to a study where, with Bible and sacramentary on one side of the desk and newspaper and literary anthology on the other, the insights gleaned from solitary wrestling with God's word appear on stationery, typescript or computer display terminal. It is true that the preacher is personally responsible for the text preached. There may be instances in which the preacher, like the prophet of old, is alone vouchsafed a divine message for the gathered worshipers. But normally one is called to proclaim the *church's* faith at liturgy, not simply one's private insights.

To assist the preacher in expressing the church's faith, FIYH recommends creating a homily preparation group. Two models for structuring such a group appear in the document:

> Involve members of the congregation in a homily preparation group. One way to begin such a group is for the preachers to invite four or five people they trust and can work with easily to join them for an hour at the beginning of the week. In a parish setting it is advisable to have one of the members drop out after four weeks and invite someone else to take his or her place. Similarly, a second will drop out after the fifth week, so that after eight weeks or so they will be working with a new group of people.
>
> A homily preparation group can also be formed by gathering the priests in the rectory, the parish staff, priests from the area, priest and ministers, or a priests' support group. The presence of members of the congregation in a group is especially helpful in raising issues that are of concern to them and which the homily may be able to address. Groups that involve

79

only clergy or parish staff members can also be a rich source of insight. (#106–7)

I support the notion of a homily preparation group, although I would probably not structure it quite as rigidly as FIYH does. My concern is that the group's membership represent a genuine cross-section of humanity and a variety of perspectives.

Genders While it would be reductionistic to suggest that there is a single feminine perspective on religious issues, one cannot deny that women may accent dimensions of revelation unnoticed or discounted by men. After Elisabeth Schüssler Fiorenza criticized one of Walter Burghardt's typically elegant Advent homilies about waiting for the Lord because, in his process of preparation, he did not ask a pregnant woman what it feels like to await the birth of her child, she asserted:

> I would suggest that in such a restrictive ecclesial situation the homilist has not just the function to articulate his own experience of God as a very particular experience but must also seek to articulate publicly the learning process and experiences of the people of God as well, since they are for the most part excluded from public proclamation. In order to be able to do so the homilist must become (1) self-critical, (2) attentive to the experience of others not like himself, (3) seek the involvement of those others in the task of preaching and proclamation, and (4) develop dialogical modes and styles of preaching.[8]

Making sure that women are members of the parish's homily preparation group should help the male preacher in these tasks.

Ages Similarly, the homily preparation group can be enriched by members of different ages. A retiree can point out the activist bias in a middle-aged preacher's presentation of Christian discipleship. A high schooler can reveal the adult hypocrisy and compromises that so often blunt the gospel's imperatives. In my experience, children are the most neglected addressees in the average homily. I suspect that many celibates overlook children's concerns in their preaching simply because children are not part of most celibates' households. I am not suggesting that grade schoolers should become part of the homily preparation group (although it might be tried as an experiment); it is more realistic for the preacher to spend time observing children in family and school settings to discover their concerns. I do not believe that every homily must explicitly address every age group, but by having people of different ages in the homily preparation group, no age's issues will be neglected in the long run.

Educational Backgrounds   There is a story told of a Quaker meeting in which a noted academic, ignoring the meditative "sense of the meeting," intruded on the communal silence with a lengthy and abstract discourse on his latest research on a gospel passage. At the conclusion of his talk one of the participants is reputed to have remarked: "The Lord promised to feed us on his word, but he didn't make us giraffes!"

The preacher must be concerned with communicating to those without college (or even high school) degrees, since the word of God addresses all humans without regard for their intellectual development. There is a danger, however, in underestimating the capacity of congregations to explore the intellectual dimensions of their faith. I have heard preachers deliberately mislead congregations by refusing to acknowledge the complexity of certain moral issues or the limitations of human language before divine mystery. When challenged, these preachers reel off platitudes about not disturbing the serenity of the "simple faithful," seemingly oblivious to their own patronizing attitudes. Testing out one's preaching ideas with members of a homily preparation team of different educational backgrounds can keep the preacher from over- or underestimating the auditors. **81**

Ethnic Heritages A sad indictment of the quality of American worship is the observation that Sunday morning church services may be the most racially segregated of all public acts. Yet one of the glories of Roman Catholic Christianity is the conviction that faith in Jesus unites people transnationally and transculturally. Having representatives of various ethnic heritages in the homily preparation group will both guard against the preacher inadvertently reinforcing cultural stereotypes and provide other perspectives on the implications of the gospel.

A perspective especially germane to initiation preaching came from a missioner in Africa who, after extensive evangelization among the members of a certain tribe, was asked by the elders to baptize the entire group. He refused, explaining that he had to be sure each of the tribe's members individually understood and was personally committed to Christianity. The elders responded: "Just because one nephew in a clan is foolish we do not cast him out of the clan. How will he become wise in the clan's ways if he does not rub shoulders with us?" From this encounter the missioner learned something both about his own cultural bias in relation to Christian conversion and about the meaning of the credal article entitled "the communion of saints."

Socio-economic Classes Finally, it would be helpful to have members of the homily preparation group represent different socio-economic classes. Examples in preaching that seem generous in one context may be petty in others. Mentions of brand-names and vacation destinations may needlessly alienate members of the assembly. Credibility of illustrative stories may hinge on awareness of customary class behavior. Sensitivity to class stratification can be increased for a preacher in conversation with those of other socio-economic backgrounds.

Declare the Hoped-for Outcomes

Every preacher has had the experience of someone remarking how meaningful she or he has found a particular homily, but when pressed for the point that seemed so powerful, the person identifies something the preacher doesn't remember saying. While it is quite possible for God to touch the hearts of auditors in ways not controlled by the preacher's intent, proposing an intended result arising from the preaching can both organize the preacher's thoughts and rhetorical strategies as well as provide criteria for evaluating the preaching's effects. Although the proximate goals of liturgical preaching may be to impart new information or to stir certain emotions, I believe that the ultimate result of liturgical preaching is to reinforce or challenge present worldviews and behaviors, or to envision new worldviews and behaviors.

Reinforcing Worldview and Behavior *Fulfilled in Your Hearing* argues that the primary task of liturgical preaching is to reinforce the "sacred canopy" of Christian belief and practice:

> Social science research contends that the oral presentation of a single person is not a particularly effective way to impart new information or to bring about a change in attitude or behavior. It is, however, well suited to make explicit or to reinforce attitudes or knowledge previously held. The homily, therefore, which normally is an oral presentation by a single person, will be less effective as a means of instruction and/or exhortation than of interpretation—that is, as a means of enabling people to recognize the implications, in liturgy and in life, of the faith that is already theirs. (#69)

This assertion implies that preaching at the eucharist when sympathizers and catechumens are present must not forsake its primary task of reinforcing the assembly's faith in order to concentrate simply on instruction. It may be helpful for the preacher to begin by emphasizing the practices and values held up by the culture that are congruent with the gospel: practices and values such as respect for the dignity of each person, concern for equal access to the goods of society, belief in informed debate to reach wise decisions, "life, liberty and the pursuit of happiness." The preacher then can show how the Christian gospel reinterprets these values (e.g., what is true life, true liberty, true happiness, and where are they to be found?) while preserving what is best about them.

Challenging Worldview and Behavior There also are times, however, when the preacher must confront values and practices that are not congruent with the gospel. For the ancient world it was clear: If one declared that Jesus the Christ was Lord, one could not give ultimate allegiance to any other reality and could not burn incense to the portrait of the emperor, even at the cost of one's life. The contemporary preacher might have to be just as direct in naming the behaviors incompatible with Christian belief.

I find it fascinating to contrast present-day catechesis—with its emphases on making the inquirer comfortable, manifesting hospitality and avoiding moral judgments—with the fierce declarations made about proper and improper behavior in documents such as the *Didache* and the *Apostolic Tradition*. Present wisdom seems to hold that we should present the Christian message as something attractive and appealing, reserving moral challenges until the auditors have bought the message. At least some communities of ancient Christians took the opposite tack: Until one had shown evidence of moral conversion, one could not hear the gospel (see, for example, the list of occupations that one had to abandon before one could be admitted as a catechumen, according to the *Apostolic Tradition*).

The initiation preacher is faced with a delicate balancing act. What is genuinely good in cultural values and personal behavior must be identified as the work of the Spirit of God in history, but unless preachers are just as clear about where cultural values and personal behavior impede the Spirit of God at work in history, there is no reason for an inquirer or a catechumen to become Christian. Frederick Buechner, in his delightful work *Telling the Truth,* suggests that often before one can preach the gospel as good news ("comedy"), one must face the bad news ("tragedy") of a world in conspiracy with evil. Anything less is to pervert gospel realism — founded in God's mercy manifest toward humanity in the cross of Christ — into sentimental optimism — founded in Enlightenment mythology about the goodness of raw human nature and its infinite perfectibility.

Envisioning a New Worldview and Behavior

Scholars recently have shown particular interest in the fact that Jesus' preaching is often cast in parables, stories taken from real life with which his auditors could immediately identify but whose narratives subvert the auditors' worldview and pose ineluctable challenges to them. The auditor is "hooked" by a parable and forced to confront fundamental assumptions about how God, self, human society and the created order interact. What begins as an anticlerical joke in the parable of the Good Samaritan ends as a profound rethinking of what it means to be neighbor and whether God can be found in the guise of a presumed enemy. What begins as a meditation on the proverbial advice to heed one's family's traditions in order to succeed in the parable of the Prodigal Son ends as a challenge to a religiosity that would substitute conformity to law for the adventure of love.

Preachers who essay this form of preaching may find themselves in trouble not only with the government but with their congregations; but preaching in parables moves beyond reinforcing or challenging existing worldview and the behaviors that accompany it to creating a new worldview and the liberating behaviors appropriate to it. (In

Buechner's terminology, if reinforcing preaches the gospel as comedy and challenging preaches the gospel as tragedy, then parabling preaches the gospel as fairy tale.) The parabolic power and danger of entertaining a new worldview is brilliantly illustrated in an interchange between Roy Cohn, a successful New York lawyer and power broker dying of AIDS, and Belize, a mulatto registered nurse (formerly a drag queen) who is attending him in the hospital, in a scene from Tony Kushner's *Angels in America. Part Two: Perestroika:*

> ROY: What's it like? After?
> BELIZE: After . . . ?
> ROY: This misery ends.
> BELIZE: Hell or heaven?
> *(Roy stares at Belize.)*
> BELIZE: Like San Francisco.
> ROY: A city. Good. I was worried . . . it'd be a garden. I hate that shit.
> BELIZE: Mmmm.
>   Big city, overgrown with weeds, but flowering weeds. On every corner a wrecking crew and something new and crooked going up catty-corner to that. Windows missing in every edifice like broken teeth, fierce gusts of gritty wind, and a gray high sky full of ravens.
> ROY: Isaiah.
> BELIZE: Prophet birds, Roy.
>   Piles of trash, but lapidary like rubies and obsidian, and diamond-colored cowspit streamers in the wind. And voting booths.
> ROY: And a dragon atop a golden horde.
> BELIZE: And everyone in Balenciaga gowns with red corsages, and big dance palaces full of music and lights and racial impurity and gender confusion.
> *(Roy laughs softly, delighted.)*
> BELIZE: And all the deities are creole, mulatto, brown as the mouths of rivers.
> *(Roy laughs again.)*
> BELIZE: Race, taste and history finally overcome. And you ain't there.
> ROY *(Happily shaking his head "no" in agreement)*: And Heaven?
> BELIZE: That was Heaven, Roy.[9]

Whatever one thinks of the language employed or the theology expressed, no one can deny the parabolic power of this interchange.

Unleash the Imagination

If preachers are to reinforce, challenge and envision worldviews and behaviors, they must cultivate their imaginations. In a helpful recent work, Thomas H. Troeger invites preachers to "come to their senses" as they forge a homily.[10] He diagnoses some of the maladies in culture and training that keep preachers from imaginative discourse and prescribes some cures for these ills. In the rest of this section I will be applying some of his suggestions to preparing initiation preaching.

Alert the Eye to Keener Sight Troeger notes that many preachers were educated to rely on print medium but that American culture is increasingly shifting to visual communication of information with techniques such as cinematic montage and headline news. While we are bombarded with imagery, we rarely stop to analyze the values promoted by these images: The fittest survive; happiness consists of limitless material acquisition; consumption is inherently good; property, wealth and power are more important than people; the newest is the best. The preacher's eye must be keen not only to critique these values but to develop nonlinear modes of communicating verbally. Ignatian imaginative exercises may help the preacher visualize biblical stories. Critically reading the ads and articles in popular journals such as *People* and *Us,* or critically analyzing the commercials interrupting the evening news and popular television shows, will sensitize the preacher to the "cover stories" that sympathizers, catechumens and candidates bring to the hearing of the Christian message.

Feel the Bodily Weight of Truth Troeger also notes that many preachers are disconnected from the somatic dimension of living. (I would add that this is especially dangerous for celibates.) He encourages preachers to enter imaginatively into the enfleshed experiences faced by various members of the congregation. What does it feel like to wait in line at the unemployment office? to sit in a jail cell? to lie on a hospital bed? to take drugs to control a mental illness? These somatic experiences can liberate new insights into the realities mirrored in scriptural narratives and the worlds that parishioners inhabit.

Listen to the Music of Speech Troeger asserts that many preachers are more attentive to the content of the words than to the words themselves. In a culture suspicious of rhetoric and deprecating of literature, few preachers consider how the sounds of words shape oral communication or how rhythm, pitch, volume and inflection reinforce or obfuscate content. I confess to a preference for Anglo-Saxon over latinate words when preaching; my written communication tends in the other direction. Although the theological content is the same, I believe it is much more powerful to hallow "God-in-our-flesh" than to proclaim "the divine incarnation," to speak of the earth as God's "dwelling" rather than God's "habitation."

Understand Resistance to Imagination Both the church and secular society tend to be suspicious of imagination, even though they acknowledge the need for it in order to live humanly. Imagination is equated with fantasy; preachers then inveigh against imagination as the enemy of truth and society marginalizes imagination as a distraction that keeps us from maximizing productivity. To cultivate the imagination is to unmask pretensions to ultimacy in the *status quo* and to risk constructing alternative worlds. Preaching at the rites of initiation frees initiates and faithful alike to dream of worlds where offended fathers hold feasts for rather than beat their sons; where enemies bind each other's wounds rather than pierce each other's bodies with bullets; where welfare recipients are waited on by CEO's; where God kneels to wash our dirty feet. The challenge then becomes living so that what we imagine shapes our world, so that the Word becomes flesh in our midst.

Return to the Source Finally, Troeger notes that many preachers lead such busy lives that they do not enter into the silence from which both imagination and the encounter with God spring. One blessing of initiation ministry is that it gently impels all those involved to return to the Source. One cannot serve as guide and companion on another's faith journey without being challenged about one's own faith. One cannot direct and encourage prayer without deepening one's own spirituality. Taking seriously the disciplines needed for initiation preaching will lead to a more contemplative stance toward life in general and a hunger for ongoing encounter with God.

Draft the Presentation

When it comes time to craft the homily, preachers must decide what form of drafting the presentation best supports their oral communication. Some preachers entirely draft their homily mentally and preach without notes. They create a "brain map" of the major points and transitions to be made and to be consulted internally as the preaching unfolds. The advantage of this form of presentation is that it guarantees that the preacher adopts a conversational style in preaching and is free to go "where the Spirit leads" during the course of the homily. Disadvantages include the possibility that the preacher will ramble on or go blank at a crucial moment, that verbal idiosyncracies will not be raised to consciousness and critiqued, or that illustrative quotations from statistics and literature will be avoided. (Some members of the congregation may suspect that the preacher has not prepared if there are no notes or written text.)

Other preachers draft homily notes, putting on a single sheet of paper or note cards an introduction, the major points being made, and a conclusion. Notes of this type preserve the preacher from memory lapses, record significant turns of phrase, and allow quotations to be cited exactly. However, using such outlines will reduce the chances that the preacher will "catch fire" in the homiletic event and may even distance him or her from the auditors.

Still other preachers write out their entire homily word-for-word. This has the advantage of allowing the preacher to craft the preaching event with the greatest degree of control, to present one's thoughts without lapses of memory or undue emphases, to polish one's prose until it communicates with clarity, vigor and delight. But writing out the homily in this manner could seduce the preacher into reading it at the congregation rather than addressing them informally, with the same lack of interest in the auditors that occurs in most academic gatherings in which formal papers are read.

However one drafts the presentation, the goal is *oral* communication with a concrete group of auditors celebrating a particular liturgical event.

Introductions During my studies in Rome, a group of fellow student priests and I shared "homiletic introductions guaranteed to disengage the congregation." Examples include: "In the gospel/first reading/second reading today, God tells us . . . ," "Have you ever wondered why we call the walkway around the church an ambulatory?" "Who can forget the glorious sight of the white smoke arising from the chimney of the Sistine

Chapel . . . ?" "When it was my good fortune to visit the Holy Land . . ." and (the first place winner!) "Although I haven't had the time to prepare, I'd just like to say . . . ."

Preachers know how important introductions are in the preaching event; because if one doesn't gain the assembly's attention at the outset, one rarely gains it later. Some preachers use the introduction to give an overview of the entire homily, believing in the old instructional adage: "Tell them what you're going to tell them, tell them, then tell them what you told them." Others try to stir the congregation's curiosity by posing a problem or asking a question. Many preachers employ stories as introductory material. Unfortunately, these stories sometimes have little or no connection with the message being preached and congregational interest disappears as soon as the story ends. When the story is about the preacher himself, it can be even more problematic: self-disclosure on the part of preachers may endear them to the congregation, but it may also focus attention more on the messenger than on the message.

Body With the humor characteristic of many seminarians, my college classmates referred to our rector's homilies as "magical mystery tours." He was a highly creative preacher, but many of us hadn't a clue about the point he was making in a given homily until the final sentence (and sometimes not even then!). Nevertheless, he held our attention as we pondered the connections he'd make between topics as diverse as synergism, Venezuelan farming practices and the description of the early Christian community in Acts. Having been given guided tours of his methods of connecting the gospel with all of life, we were encouraged to do the same.

The body of a homily could be organized in any number of ways. Some preachers choose to follow the narrative of a given reading proclaimed at that liturgy.

They retell the story in such a way that its implications for contemporary auditors become clear. Much classic African American preaching uses this storytelling format: The preacher role-plays the various biblical characters, and the congregation verbally and gesturally indicates its recognition of the story's contemporary relevance. Other preachers begin with the life experience of the congregation, probe it for its connection to the scriptures proclaimed and the event celebrated, and lead the assembly to praise and thank God for God's action in their lives. No matter how it is organized, the body of the homily must bring together the biblical/liturgical heritage and witness, the real lives of the congregation and the preacher's witness. Salvation *history* must be claimed as *our story* by one who credibly acknowledges it as *my story.*

Conclusion Homilies should conclude, not simply end. Some preachers move in their preaching from talking about God to talking to God, moving from an address to the assembly to a concluding pastoral prayer. This could be especially effective when the preacher makes it a practice to sit with the worshiping assembly in meditative silence for some minutes after the spoken prayer concludes. Other preachers tie the conclusion of the homily to the opening of the Creed: "Having heard and pondered God's word to us today, let us together stand and profess our faith." On occasion one might yoke the conclusion of the homily with text of a "hymn of the day" that the congregation will be asked to sing. Sometimes texts of liturgical prayer (phrases from the proper preface, a eucharistic prayer or a congregational acclamation) may provide a powerful conclusion.

When catechumens are to be dismissed, the preacher has a wonderful opportunity to conclude by speaking directly to them, their sponsors and their catechists. In a few sentences they can be commissioned to ponder more deeply the central assertions of the homily. Such a charge would lead quite naturally into intercessory prayer for them and their formal dismissal.

Practice the Preaching

Having drafted the presentation, the final act of the preacher is to practice its delivery. Practicing the homily will point up necessary revisions.

Oral Communication Because the homily is a form of oral communication, preachers must aim at the ear rather than the eye. Simple declarations and questions should be preferred to prolix compound, complex sentences. Strong verbs and nouns will carry thought much more effectively than multiple adjectives or relative clauses. Euphony and balance of elements can all enhance oral communication.

Amplification of the speaker's voice must also be considered an element in oral communication. If microphones are used, the preacher should chart a course between ignoring the amplification and relying on it to carry the sound. The preacher should project the voice without shouting or straining, avoiding common problems such as swallowing the ends of phrases, using a singsong alternation of pitches or adopting a pietistic tone.

Language Register and Vocabulary Unless preachers are striving for particular rhetorical effects, they should also steer a middle ground between elevated discourse and slang. Technical ("Jesus is the eschatological sign and the proleptic anticipation of the consummation of God's Reign"), pretentious ("our most puissant and omnipotent deity") or hackneyed ("holy mother church") language impedes effective homiletic communication. Vigorous and expressive "ordinary" language, the language and most people in the congregation would use in public, provides the surest guide to both register and vocabulary. The preacher should not be afraid, however, to employ heightened speech, especially to create an arresting conclusion.

Gestures Some preachers give the impression that they are "brains-on-a-stick," that their bodies are not involved in the message their mouths are announcing. Others develop gestural tics such as rocking back and forth, swaying from side to side, jabbing the air with an index finger or (horrors!) scratching themselves. These mannerisms are usually unconscious but can be controlled if brought to the preacher's attention. Still other preachers produce gestures to convey particular emotions with all the subtlety and grace of a marionette.

The Bauhaus principle of architecture, "less is more," applies when considering gesture in the homily. A few well-chosen moves coordinated with the principal emphases of the preaching communicate more effectively than a barrage of undisciplined movements.

As we conclude this chapter on preparing liturgical preaching for the rites of initiation, FIYH provides some fitting words of advice and encouragement:

> The preacher . . . has a formidable task: to speak from the scriptures (those inspired documents of our tradition that hand down to us the way the first believers interpreted the world) to a gathered congregation in such a way that those assembled will be able to worship God in spirit and truth, and then go forth to love and serve the Lord. But while the task is formidable, it is not impossible, especially if one goes about it with purpose and method.

Chapter 4

Approaches to Initiation Preaching from Ancient Christian Writers

■

Much of the information liturgical historians have been able to recover concerning the initiation practices of the post-apostolic church comes from addresses preached at those events. Careful analysis of these texts reveals not only the diversity of initiation practice in different parts of the world but also the variety of styles of initiation preaching. Contemporary preachers will find both a wealth of information and models worthy of imitation in the initiation preaching of the patristic period.[1]

Admittedly, the conditions these preachers engaged are far removed both in time and locale from contemporary situations in North America. The assumptions made by preachers and auditors alike about the universe and humanity's place in it were quite different from ours. Their social structures were different, their prized forms of rhetoric disparate, their philosophical categories diverse. Perhaps most importantly, their approach to the

95

scriptures was not informed by contemporary varieties of historical and literary criticism.

Nevertheless, I believe that patristic initiation preaching can teach us much. It provides us not so much with texts to be quoted as with approaches to be emulated. Thus rather than present a chronological or geographical survey in this chapter, I will identify five approaches taken by patristic preachers and illustrate how one might hallow cosmic symbols, explore anthropological patterns, celebrate biblical history, analyze belief and behavior, and/ or reveal the future present in initiation preaching. (Translations of the patristic texts have been modified to reflect the contemporary concern for inclusivity in language.)

Hallowing Cosmic Symbols

Much patristic initiation preaching keenly observes the natural world. For these preachers and their hearers, astronomical phenomena, the ceaseless round of the seasons, the practices of animals and the properties of material objects all bespeak deeper realities. The preacher's task is to identify nature's analogues to the initiation process and to evoke a sense of wonder at the cosmic importance of the ritual events.

Melito, a native of the city of Sardis who may have served as its bishop around the years 160 to 170, vividly explores astronomical symbolism in conjunction with Christian baptism in a fragmentary homily:

> If you wish to observe the heavenly bodies being baptized, make haste now to the Ocean, and there I will show you a strange sight: outspread sea, and boundless main, and infinite deep, and immeasurable Ocean, and pure water: the sun's swimming-pool, and the stars' brightening-place, and the moon's bath. . . . When the sun has with fiery chariotry fulfilled the day's course . . . he sinks into the Ocean. . . . And when he has bathed in symbolic baptism, he exults greatly, taking the water as food. Though one and the same, he rises

for [us] as a new sun, tempered from the deep, purified from the bath; he has driven off the nocturnal darkness, and has begotten bright day. Along his course, both the movement of the stars and the appearance of the moon operate. For they bathe in the sun's swimming-pool like good disciples; for the stars with the moon pursue the sun's track, soaking up pure brilliance.

Now if the sun, with stars and moon, bathes in the Ocean, why may not Christ also bathe in Jordan? King of heavens and creation's Captain, Sun of uprising who appeared both to the dead in Hades and to mortals in the world, he alone arose a Sun out of heaven.[2]

Note Melito's imagery: He graphically evokes for his hearers the common experience of watching a sunset, yet his language leads them to connect this cosmic event with the experience of Christian initiation. Just as moon and stars are purified in the "sun's swimming-pool" made radiant by contact with the sun's fiery presence, so Christians are purified in the baptismal waters made radiant by contact with Christ's body in the Jordan River. (There may even be a reference to the neophyte's drinking of the baptismal water at the initiation eucharist in the image of the sun "taking the water as food.") While Melito's understanding of the universe with the earth at its center would not be shared by contemporary first-world people, his creativity in yoking cosmic "baptism" with Christian baptism could be emulated.

Ephrem the Syrian (c. 306 – 373), noted for his *madrashe* (stanzaic instructional hymns intended for choral singing) and *memre* (non-stanzaic metrical homilies intended for recitation), contrasts in his *Hymn on Virginity* 7 two months as a symbol of the two worlds Christians inhabit: this world of space and time (October) and the world of the Easter mystery (April):

October gives rest to the weary after the dust and dirt
    of the summer,
its rain washes, its dew anoints the trees and their fruit.
April gives rest to the fasters, it anoints, baptizes
    and clothes in white;

it cleanses off the dirt of sin from our souls.
October presses out the oil for us,
    April multiplies mercies for us;
In October fruit is gathered, in April sins are forgiven.³

Because the period of purification and enlightenment
is normatively situated in Lent, sacramental initiation
situated during the Easter Vigil and mystagogia during
the fifty days of Eastertide, preachers in the Northern
hemisphere could easily draw connections with the seasonal rebirth of nature. Lengthening periods of sunshine,
fresh breezes, lakes and ponds melting and trees in bud
all provide natural springboards for initiation preaching.

Ambrose of Milan (c. 333/339 – 397), whose preaching was so powerful as to bring Augustine to Christian
baptism, presents a delightful comparison between the
behavior of fish and the activities of the baptized in his
On the Sacraments 3:

> You have read about water, "Let the waters brings forth crea-
> tures having life" [Genesis 1:20 – 21], and creatures having life
> were born. They indeed were in the beginning of creation,
> but for you it was reserved for water to regenerate you unto
> grace, just as water generated other creatures unto life. Imitate
> the fish, which indeed has obtained less grace, yet should be
> an object of wonder to you. It is in the sea and is upon the
> waters; it is in the sea and swims upon the floods. A tempest
> rages in the sea, storms shriek, but the fish swims; it is not
> submerged, because it is accustomed to swim. So even for you
> this world is a sea. It has diverse floods, heavy waters, severe
> storms. And do you be a fish, that the water of the world may
> not submerge you.⁴

Especially in rural settings and with congregations who
are familiar with agricultural life, the behavior of animals
(birds migrating to their winter homes, fish driven to
return to a particular place to spawn, sheep huddling in
a flock) may spark the preacher's imagination and provide a bond with the preacher's audience.

Gregory of Nyssa (c. 335 – 394), in a homily that he
prepared for the feast of the Epiphany and that he most

likely preached on 6 January 383, explores the transformative properties of material objects employed by the Holy Spirit:

> It is not the water that bestows this gift . . . but the command of God and the visitation of the Spirit that comes sacramentally to set us free. But water serves to express the cleansing. For since we are wont by washing in water to render our body clean when it is soiled by dirt or mud, we therefore apply it also in the sacramental action, and display the spiritual brightness by that which is subject to our senses. . . . [The human], as we know full well, is compound, not simple; and therefore the cognate and similar medicines are assigned for healing to [this one] who is twofold and conglomerate: for [the] visible body, water, the sensible element, for [the] soul, which we cannot see, the Spirit invisible, invoked by faith, present unspeakably. . . . Despise not, therefore, the divine laver, not think lightly of it, as a common thing, on account of the use of water. For the power that operates is mighty, and wonderful are the things that are wrought thereby.
>
> For this holy altar, too, by which I stand, is stone, ordinary in its nature, no way different from the other slabs of stone that build our houses and adorn our pavements; but seeing that it was consecrated to the service of God, and received the benediction, it is a holy table, an altar undefiled, no longer touched by the hands of all, but of the priests alone, and that with reverence. The bread again is at first common bread, but when the sacramental action consecrates it, it is called, and becomes, the Body of Christ. So with the sacramental oil; so with the wine: though before the benediction they are of little value, each of them, after the sanctification bestowed by the Spirit, has its several functions. . . . Now, by a similar train of reasoning, water also, though it is nothing else than water, renews the [human] to spiritual regeneration, when the grace from above hallows it.[5]

Contemporary preachers may likewise wish to explore the physical properties of the core symbols that are used in the rites of Christian initiation. Olive oil that flavors pasta, soothes strained muscles and provides wicks with flammable matter; wax candles that can only provide warmth and illumination by being used up; perfume that bespeaks sophistication, attracts lovers, and sets off allergic reactions — all could be examined as natural elements revealing the sacramental character of God's world.

A major difficulty for contemporary preachers in employing cosmic symbolism in initiation preaching is the "cover story" presumed by those educated in the physical sciences. We have passed from geocentric through heliocentric to random and relativistic views of the universe, making it difficult for many contemporary Christians to find symbolic resonance in astronomical phenomena. Similarly, we tend to be empiricists, locating the "really real" in what is able to be sensed and quantified, which is in contrast to the neo-Platonic philosophic underpinnings of much patristic thinking, where the transitory and perishable concrete is nothing but a pale reflection of its "really real" Form. We late twentieth-century Christians would consider the early twentieth-century Joseph Michael Plunkett's lyrical evocation of the cosmic Christ a poetic fancy rather than a revelatory disclosure:

> I see his blood upon the rose
> And in the stars the glory of his eyes,
> His body gleams amid eternal snows,
> His tears fall from the skies.
>
> I see his face in every flower;
> The thunder and the singing of the birds
> Are but his voice — and carven by his power
> Rocks are his written words.
>
> All pathways by his feet are worn,
> His strong heart stirs the ever-beating sea,
> His crown of thorns is twined with every thorn,
> His cross is every tree.

But "ecotheologians" such as Thomas Berry,[6] Brian Swimme[7] and Sallie McFague[8] are challenging mechanistic understandings of the universe in ways that may help contemporary preachers recover with their congregations a sense of God's pervading presence in the very structure and unfolding of the world.

Exploring Anthropological Patterns

In addition to yoking symbols of nature with Christian initiation, patristic preaching revels in comparisons and contrasts between elements of human culture and the events of the initiation process. As one might expect, parallels between human birth and spiritual rebirth have pride of place, but images drawn from many other human experiences also appear.

Theodore of Mopsuestia, a fellow student of rhetoric and theology with John Chrysostom and a bishop in Cilicia from 392 until his death in 428, explores the relationship between human conception and development with the effects of baptism in his *Baptismal Homily* 3:

> Just as in natural birth the mother's womb receives a seed, but it is God's hand that forms it according to his original decree, so too in baptism the water becomes a womb to receive the person who is being born, but it is the grace of the Spirit which forms [that one] there for a second birth and makes . . . a completely new [person]. A seed settling in the mother's womb has neither life nor soul nor sense; but God's hand forms it so that it emerges a living [human], endowed with soul and senses and a nature capable of any human action. So too here: the one baptized settles in the water as in a kind of womb, like a seed showing no sign of an immortal nature; but once baptized and endowed with the divine grace of the Spirit, [human] nature is reshaped completely. Once mortal, it becomes immortal; once corruptible, it becomes incorruptible; once changing, it becomes unchanging: by the almighty power of [the one] who forms it. . . .
>
> A baby born of a woman has the potentiality of talking, hearing, walking and working with his hands, but is too utterly weak for any action of the kind; yet, in due time, by God's decree he becomes capable of these actions. So too one who is born by baptism possesses . . . all the potentialities of [our] immortal and incorruptible nature, but cannot use or exhibit them until the moment God has ordained for us to be born from the dead and attain full enjoyment of our freedom from corruption, death, pain and change. We are endowed with the potentiality for these things at baptism but gain the

effective use of them only when we are no longer merely natural but spiritual, and the working of the Spirit has made the body incorruptible and the soul immutable, holding them both in [God's] own power and preserving them.[9]

This parallel between physical and spiritual birth and development reaches a high point in Thomas Aquinas' sacramental theology, which argues that it is fitting that there be seven sacraments on the basis of a certain correspondence between corporal and spiritual life (cf. *Summa Theologiae* III.5.1.Resp.). Although contemporary sacramental theologians might object that this reasoning leads to recasting confirmation as a sacrament of maturity, contemporary preachers may still want to advert to the resemblances between physical birth and baptism.

Zeno, who served as bishop of Verona from c. 360 to 380, strongly contrasts natural childbirth with spiritual generation at baptism in one of his "Invitations to the Font":

Exult, brothers [and sisters] in Christ, and hastening by every desire receive heavenly gifts. Now the saving warmth of the eternal font invites you. Now our Mother adopts you so that she might give birth to you. But [you are to be born] not by that law by which your mothers brought you forth — mothers groaning in the pain of childbirth, bringing you forth weeping, sullied and wrapped in soiled swaddling clothes to the miseries of this world — but with you rejoicing in happiness, heavenly [children], free from all sins, to be nurtured not in foul-smelling cradles but at the railings of the sacred altar with sweet-smelling perfumes. Through our Lord Jesus Christ.[10]

While contemporary preachers might not want to evoke the pangs of childbirth and the odors of diapers quite so intensely, the unflinching realism of Zeno's prose powerfully yokes common human experience with transcendent meaning. (They may also want to examine other of Zeno's "invitations to the font" as models for short but powerful *monitiones* interspersed throughout the initiation rites.)

John Chrysostom, in his *Baptismal Homily* 2 preached in the Constantinian basilica of Antioch about two weeks before Easter in 390, illuminates the meaning of the pre-baptismal exorcisms by reference to court etiquette:

> You need to know why it is that after the daily instruction we send you off to hear the words of the exorcists. This rite is neither a simple one nor pointless. You are about to receive the heavenly King into your house. So those who are appointed for this task, just as if they were preparing a house for a royal visit, take you on one side after our sermon, and purify your minds by those fearful words, putting to flight all the tricks of the Evil One, and so make the house fit for the presence of the King. . . .
>
> The wonderful, unbelievable thing is that every difference and distinction of rank is missing here. If anyone happens to be in a position of worldly importance or conspicuous wealth, if he boasts of his birth or the glory of this present life, he stands on just the same footing as the beggar in rags, the blind [one] or the lame. Nor does he complain at this since he knows that all such differences have been set aside in the life of the spirit; a grateful heart is the only requirement.[11]

Chrysostom's vision of Christian egalitarianism in a strongly hierarchical society could challenge contemporary preachers to ponder how Christ should be received by people misformed by North American traits of economic stratification and rugged individualism.

Ambrose of Milan looks to contract law to illustrate the implications of the rite of renunciation in his *On the Sacraments* 1:

> Be mindful of your words, and never let the sequence of your bond be broken. If you give [someone] surety, you are held responsible, so that you may receive [that person's] money; you are held bound, and the lender binds you if your resist. If you refuse, you go to a judge and there you will be convicted by your own bond.
>
> Consider where you promised, or to whom you promised. You saw the Levite [deacon], but he is the minister of Christ. You saw him minister before the altar. Therefore, your surety is held, not on earth, but in heaven.[12]

Would a contemporary preacher feel equally free to describe the practices of pawn shops or the inexorable mechanisms of the IRS in depicting the force of the pledges made during Christian initiation? (On the other hand, our increasingly litigious society seems to have less and less respect for legal practitioners and more and more despair of finding true justice within the system, which may make the use of legal analogies problematic.)

Augustine of Hippo, addressing the newly baptized of the city where he served as bishop on Easter morning, weaves an extended reflection on the eucharist as sacrament of unity by exploring the process by which bread is baked in his *Sermon 227*:

> By bread you are instructed as to how you ought to cherish unity. Was that bread made of one grain of wheat? Were there not, rather, many grains? However, before they became bread, these grains were separate; they were joined together in water after a certain amount of crushing. For, unless the grain is ground and moistened with water, it cannot arrive at that form which is called bread. So, too, you were previously ground, as it were, by the humiliation of your fasting and by the sacrament of exorcism. Then came the baptism of water; you were moistened, as it were, so as to arrive at the form of bread. But, without fire, bread does not yet exist. What, then, does the fire signify? The chrism. For the sacrament of the Holy Spirit is the oil of our fire. . . . The Holy Spirit will come on Pentecost. And thus he will come: he will show himself in tongues of fire. For he kindles charity by which we ardently desire God and spurn the world, by which our chaff is consumed and our heart is purified as gold. Therefore, the fire, that is, the Holy Spirit, comes after the water; then you become bread, that is, the body of Christ. Hence, in a certain manner, unity is signified.[13]

The more that contemporary preachers are in touch with the domestic lives of their hearers, the wider will be the field of appropriate examples. In a world where few knead their daily bread, Augustine's extended reflection on bread-baking might seem quaint. But there may be parallel possibilities for the contemporary preacher based on an exploration of computer games, popular music, television programs, etc.

The freedom with which patristic preachers ranged through the human behaviors in their cultures to find analogues to Christian ritual behavior should encourage contemporary preachers to enter into a similar engagement with their own culture. They might want to explore the parallels between conferring citizenship on immigrants and the process of Christian initiation. The ordeals involved in getting a driver's license (involving both theoretical and practical knowledge) may provide counterparts to the catechumenal rites. Opening a bank account, getting a credit card or paying one's taxes for the first time could correlate with phases of Christian initiation. Military service, apprenticeship at a job, or betrothal and marriage preparation may all provide comparisons to the "rites of passage" in Christian initiation. Contemporary preachers ignore the impact of secular culture to their peril.

Celebrating Biblical History

As appealing as hallowing cosmic symbols and exploring anthropological patterns is in patristic preaching, one must admit that at their core these texts are celebrations of biblical history. Patristic preaching is steeped in citations and allusions from both the Old and New Testaments and is frequently explicated in terms of typology (contrasts between "figures," "shadows" or "images" and their corresponding "realities," "substances" or "truths") or allegory (decoding of encrypted correspondences). While patristic treatment of the sacred scripture might be considered eisegetical, fanciful or arbitrary by contemporary standards, it clearly presumes that the biblical narrative provides a "sacred canopy" under which the meaning of human life can be consecrated. What follows is a sampling of how various patristic preachers treated some of the archetypal scriptural passages associated with Christian initiation: the creation, the flood, the exodus from Egypt, the crossing of the Jordan under Joshua's leadership and the cleansing of Naaman from the Old Testament, plus the baptism of Jesus and the opening of Christ's side from the New Testament.

Contained in Agathangelos' *History of the Armenians* is a text titled *The Teaching of St. Gregory,* which appears to be a catechism written about 440. Though not strictly a homily, the text reprises many of the patristic themes connecting the Genesis accounts of creation with Christian initiation:

> Because [God] made the first earth emerge from the waters by [divine] command, and by water were fattened all plants and reptiles and wild animals and beasts and birds, and by the freshness of the waters they sprang up from the earth; in the same way by baptism [God] made verdant the womb of generation of the waters, purifying by the waters and renewing the old deteriorated earthy matter, which sin had weakened and enfeebled and deprived of the grace of the Spirit. Then the invisible Spirit opened again the womb by visible water, preparing the newly born fledglings for the regeneration of the font, to clothe all with robes of light who would be born once more.
>
> For in the beginning of the creation of time, the Spirit of the Deity moved over the waters, and thence set out the order of the creatures, and commanded the coming into being and establishing of the creatures. [This Spirit] also ordered to be established the firmament of heaven, the dwelling of the fiery angels, which appears to us as water. In the same way [the spirit] came and completed the covenant made with our [ancestors. God] came down to the waters and sanctified the lower waters of this earth, which had been fouled by the sins of [humankind].
>
> Treading the waters with his own footsteps, [Jesus] sanctified them and made them purifying. And just as formerly the Spirit moved over the waters, in the same way [the Spirit] will dwell in the waters and will receive all who are born by it. And the waters massed together above are the dwelling of the angels. But [God] made these waters just as those, because he

himself came down to the waters, that all might be renewed through the Spirit by the waters and become angels, and the same Spirit might bring all to adoption by the waters forever. For he opened the gates of the waters below, that the gates of the upper waters of heaven might be opened, and that he might elevate all [humankind] in glory to adoption.[14]

Tertullian (c. 155/160–240/250) is noted as the author of the earliest treatise on baptism in East or West, having written his *Homily on Baptism* between 200 and 206. Chapter eight of the work explores in typological fashion the imposition of hands after postbaptismal chrismation in North African initiation rites and the gift of the Holy Spirit, foreshadowed in the dove returning to Noah's ark:

> After those waters of the Flood by which the ancient iniquity had been washed away, after the baptism (so to express it) of the world, a dove as herald announced to the earth peace from the wrath of heaven, and having returned with an olive-leaf—and toward the heathen too this is held out as a sign of peace—by the same [divine] ordinance of spiritual effectiveness the dove who is the Holy Spirit is sent forth from heaven, where the church is which is the type of the ark, and flies down bringing God's peace to the earth which is our flesh, as it comes up from the washing after [the removal of] its ancient sins. "But," [you object,] "the world sinned once more, so that this equating of baptism with the flood is not valid." [The world sinned], and so is appointed for the fire, as also a [person] is [who] renews his sins after baptism: so that this also needs to be accepted as a sign and a warning to us.[15]

Cyril, bishop of Jerusalem from 349 to 389, masterfully celebrates biblical history by contrasting the "figure" of the Exodus from Egypt with the "reality" of the rite of renunciation and profession in his *First Lecture on the Mysteries:*

> First you entered the antechamber of the baptistry and faced towards the west. On the command to stretch out your hand, you renounced Satan as though he were there in person. This moment, you should know, is prefigured in ancient history. When that tyrannous and cruel despot, Pharaoh, was oppressing the noble, free-spirited Hebrew nation, God sent Moses to deliver them from the hard slavery imposed upon them by

the Egyptians. The doorposts were anointed with the blood of a lamb that the destroyer might pass over the houses signed with the blood; so the Jews were miraculously liberated. After their liberation the enemy gave chase, and, on seeing the sea part miraculously before them, still continued in hot pursuit, only to be instantaneously overwhelmed and engulfed in the Red Sea.

Pass, pray, from the old to the new, from the figure to the reality. There Moses sent by God to Egypt; here Christ sent from the Father into the world. Moses' mission was to lead out from Egypt a persecuted people; Christ's, to rescue all the people of the world who were under the tyranny of sin. There the blood of a lamb was the charm against the destroyer; here, the blood of the unspotted Lamb, Jesus Christ, is appointed your inviolable sanctuary against demons. Pharaoh pursued that people of old right into the sea; this outrageous spirit, the impudent author of all evil, followed you, each one, up to the very verge of the saving streams. That other tyrant is engulfed and drowned in the Red Sea; this one is destroyed in the saving water.[16]

Aphrahat, a Syriac-speaking Persian who may have served as a bishop for a Christian community in fourth-century Mesopotamia, wrote his *Demonstration* 11 "On Circumcision" in 344. Playing on the fact that Joshua, Moses' successor, and Jesus share a common name in Hebrew/Aramaic/Syriac, the author presents an extended comparison between the two figures as a masterful example of typological thinking:

Joshua the son of Nun circumcised the people a second time with knives of stone when he and his people crossed the Jordan. Joshua [Jesus] our redeemer a second time circumcised the peoples who believed in him with the circumcision of the hearts, and they were baptized and circumcised with "the knife which is his word that is sharper than the two-edged sword" [Hebrews 4:12]. Joshua the son of Nun led the people across to the Land of Promise; and Joshua our redeemer promised the land of the living to whoever passed through the true Jordan, believed, and circumcised the foreskin of his heart. Joshua the son of Nun raised up stones as a testimony in Israel; and Joshua our redeemer called Simon the true stone and set him up as a faithful testimony among the peoples. Joshua the son of Nun made a Paschal sacrifice in the camp at Jericho in the cursed land . . . and the people ate from the bread of the land; and Joshua our redeemer made a Paschal sacrifice with his disciples in Jerusalem, the city which he cursed . . . saying: "There should not remain in it stone on stone" [Matthew 24:2], and there he gave them the mystery in the bread of life. Joshua the son of Nun condemned the avaricious Achan who stole and hid, and Joshua our redeemer condemned the avaricious Judas who stole and hid money from the purse which he was holding. Joshua the son of Nun wiped out unclean peoples; and Joshua our redeemer threw down Satan and his host. Joshua the son of Nun held up the sun in the sky; and Joshua our redeemer brought on sunset at noon when they crucified him. Joshua the son of Nun was redeemer of the people. Jesus was called redeemer of the peoples. Blessed are those whose hearts are circumcised from the foreskin and who are born through water, the second circumcision, for they are inheritors with Abraham, the head of believers and father of all peoples, whose faith was reckoned for him as righteousness.[17]

Gregory of Nyssa, in his *Homily for the Feast of Lights* mentioned above, provides numerous Old Testament figures of baptism (e.g., Hagar and Ishmael saved by water from a divinely revealed well, Jacob watering Rachel's flock, the infant Moses adrift in the Nile, the Israelite people passing through the Red Sea, the fire kindled by God on watered wood at the prayer of Elijah) in addition to this reference to the cleansing of Naaman:

> Yes, and yet again his [i.e., Elijah's] disciple, Elisha, when Naaman the Syrian, who was diseased with leprosy, had come to him as a suppliant, cleanses the sick man by washing him in Jordan, clearly indicating what was to come, both by the use of water generally, and by the dipping in the river in particular. For Jordan alone of rivers, receiving in itself the firstfruits of sanctification and benediction, conveyed in its channel to the whole world, as it were from some fount in the type afforded by itself, the grace of baptism.[18]

Extending the Old Testament symbolism of the Jordan River to the baptism of Christ in his *Third Lecture on the Mysteries,* Cyril of Jerusalem presents the "figure" **109** of postbaptismal anointing with the "reality" of Christ's mystical anointing at his baptism:

> He bathed in the river Jordan and, after imparting the fragrance of his Godhead to the waters, came up from them. Him the Holy Spirit visited in essential presence, like resting upon like. Similarly for you, after you had ascended from the sacred streams, there was an anointing with chrism, the antitype of that with which Christ was anointed, that is, of the Holy Spirit. . . .
>
> For Christ, was not anointed by [mortals] with material oil or balsam; his Father, appointing him Savior of the whole world, anointed him with the Holy Spirit. . . . As Christ was really crucified and buried and rose again, and you at baptism are privileged to be crucified, buried, and raised along with him in a likeness, so also with the chrism. Christ was anointed with a mystical oil of gladness; that is, with the Holy Spirit, called "oil of gladness" because he is the cause of spiritual gladness; so you, being anointed with the ointment, have become partakers and fellows of Christ.[19]

Chapter sixteen of Tertullian's *Homily on Baptism* distinguishes a "baptism of water" from a "baptism of blood" on the basis of a typological reading of John 19:34:

> We have indeed a second washing. It too a single one, that of blood, of which our Lord said, *I have a baptism to be baptized with* [Luke 12:50], when he had already been baptized. For he had come by water and blood, as John has written [1 John 5:6], so as to be baptized with water and glorified with blood. Likewise so as to give us our vocation by water and our election by blood [cf. Matthew 22:14], he sent forth these two baptisms from out of the wound of his pierced side [cf. John 19:34], because those who had faith in his blood were to be washed in water, and those who had washed in water would need also [to be washed] in blood. This is the baptism which makes actual a washing which has not been received, and gives back again one that has been lost.[20]

Two issues confront contemporary preachers in attempting to imitate the celebration of biblical history enshrined in patristic texts such as these. First of all, unlike their ancient counterparts, many members of present-day liturgical assemblies are simply ignorant of the scriptural stories. One wag has suggested that the liturgical announcement "A reading from the book of N." might just as well be replaced by "A reading from the back of a baseball card" for all the effect that knowledge of the location of a pericope has on the listening assembly. Although some thirty years ago the *Constitution on the Sacred Liturgy* declared that "sacred scripture is of the greatest importance in the celebration of the liturgy" and that "to achieve the reform, progress and adaptation of the liturgy, it is essential to promote that warm and living love for Scripture to which the venerable tradition of both Eastern and Western rites gives testimony" (#24), very few communities (outside of houses of formation, monasteries or religious communities) could boast members who would be familiar with the references behind the comparison of the two Joshuas in the selection from Aphrahat quoted earlier. Thus, while the homily is never to be reduced simply to notional instruction, I believe that it is always appropriate for the preacher to share some Bible study with the auditors, if only to whet their appetite for more formal study outside the liturgical assembly.

Second, outmoded approaches to scripture cripple contemporary preaching. In a recent work, James Dunning identifies four common approaches to scripture taken by contemporary preachers: fundamentalist/literalist, historicist, doctrinal/psychological and pastoral/theological. The first treats scripture as unvarnished history, refusing to recognize its character as a faith-document and the astonishing variety of literary genres it contains. The second takes seriously the historical character of the documents, but tends to exploit them for their picture of an ancient civilization rather than for their ability to engender faith in contemporary hearers. The third plays into contemporary biases that the scriptures are primarily addressed to individuals for their psychological comfort or are poetically palatable repositories of doctrinal axioms. In Dunning's opinion, the fourth approach, with its

111

emphasis on the literary character of the scriptural witness and its ability to call for communal conversion, is the most viable approach for contemporary preaching.[21] Thus while taking seriously the patristic celebration of biblical history, today's preacher will approach the scriptures with theories of interpretation that are more self-consciously elaborated.[22]

Analyzing Beliefs and Behaviors

Although patristic preaching hallows cosmic symbolism, engages human culture and celebrates the scriptural heritage, it is not afraid to appeal to the mind and to the will. Initiation preaching frequently asserts Christian truth claims, clarifying what Christians believe and defending those beliefs against challenges from other religious traditions and movements. Initiation preaching also prescribes Christian behavior, both condemning attitudes and actions that militate against the Christian vision of reality as well as encouraging demeanors and deeds that sustain that vision.

An anonymous preacher operating in northern Italy c. 450 (possibly around Verona) illustrates how initiation preaching clarifies the core beliefs of Christians:

> No one, however, when [hearing] "the Father and the Son and the Holy Spirit" should think that we profess three gods. May that sacrilege be far from our faith, we who know that God is one, as he himself testifies! "I," he says, "am God, and there is no other but me, there is no just and saving one but me. Turn yourselves to me and you will be saved, for from the end of the earth I am God, and there is no other but me" [Isaiah 45:21–22]. And in another book: "Hear, Israel, the Lord your God is one Lord" [Deuteronomy 6:4]. And again: "He is the Lord your God in the heaven above and on the earth below and there is no other but him" [Deuteronomy 4:39].
>
> Therefore we hold and believe in three persons (that is, the Father and the Son and the Holy Spirit) of one power, one substance, one eternity, one will, and one deity; and we ven-

erate the entire Trinity with the name of one God. To believe in many gods is pagan impiety; and again not to believe in three persons of one substance in a single, equal, and co-eternal deity is heretical madness, when the authority of Christ is manifest in the quotation that we have said: "Baptize all nations in the name of the Father and of the Son and of the Holy Spirit" [Matthew 28:19].[23]

This preacher is not afraid to employ the philosophical vocabulary of his day to present Christian beliefs with as much linguistic precision as possible; nor is he afraid to engage his opponents' positions. Interestingly, however, his technical vocabulary is limited, hallowed by tradition and contextualized by scripture. There is no room for erudition for its own sake or for intellectual titillation of the auditors. While doctrinal content appears in all preaching, proclamation of Christian doctrine may be especially appropriate when preaching at the presentations of the Creed and the Lord's Prayer.

A recurring theme in patristic initiation preaching is that belief is to guide behavior. The Christian life engendered in baptism is a matter not merely of doctrinal orthodoxy but of proper behavior. Such a conviction led patristic preachers both to excoriate practices unworthy of Christians and to exhort the baptized to particular forms of conduct.

Cyril of Jerusalem, in his *First Lecture on the Mysteries,* is forthright in condemning behaviors that are to be rejected by those who celebrate the rite of renunciation:

> Next you say, "and all his pomp." The pomp of the Devil is the craze for the theater, the horse races in the circus, the wild-beast hunts, and all such vanity, from which the saint prays to God to be delivered in the words, "Turn away mine eyes that they may not behold vanity." Avoid an addiction to the theater, with its spectacle of the licentiousness, the lewd and unseemly antics of actors and the frantic dancing of degenerates. Not for you, either, the folly of those who, to gratify their miserable appetite, expose themselves to wild beasts in the combats in the amphitheater. They pamper their belly at the cost of becoming themselves; of these gladiators it

is fair to say that in the service of the belly which is their god they court death in the arena. Shun also the bedlam of the races, a spectacle in which souls as well as riders come to grief. All these follies are the pomp of the devil. . . .

After this you say, "and all your service." The service of the Devil is prayer in the temples of idols, the honoring of lifeless images, the lighting of lamps or the burning of incense by springs or streams; there have been cases of persons who, deceived by dreams or by evil spirits, have gone to this length in the hope of being rewarded by the cure of even bodily ailments. Have nothing to do with these practices. The observation of birds, divination, omens, charms and amulets, magic and similar chicanery — all such practices are the cult of the Devil. Shun them.[24]

One wonders if contemporary preachers would be as candid in naming the "works and pomps" of the devil in today's society: dog-eat-dog competition, lust for possessions, irresponsible use of drugs and alcohol, sexism, racism, etc. Yet initiation preaching (especially at the time of the scrutinies) calls for just such bold naming of the "principalities and powers" opposed to the life of the gospel.

The "Verona Anonymous" is just as straightforward in extrapolating a general behavioral stance from the ritual foot-washing that was part of the initiation ceremonies in his community:

Having finished all the sacramental ceremonies, we also handed over to you the *mandatum* by example and by word: for we washed the feet of each of you, calling you forth to our imitation of our Lord and Savior himself, so that you would also wash the feet of your brothers and guests. Thus we would teach you not only to be hospitable, but also humbly hospitable, so that you would accept them whom you honor in your hospitality [and] so that you would not be ashamed to fulfill the office of slaves for them.

If anyone should think that this is injurious to themselves, and puffed up by devilish pride should disdain to perform the Lord's *mandatum,* and, although he is of noble stature in this age, is ashamed to wash the feet of a poor and contemptible Christian in this world, that person is ashamed of Christ who both commanded and did this act (or rather who deigned to do it before he commanded it): if indeed he set the example before us, it was so that the command might be more easily remembered. . . .

Therefore consider, brothers most beloved, of what unhappiness and what madness it would be for the slave to disdain to wash feet for a fellow-slave or a disciple for a fellow-disciple, when the Lord and Master of all deigned to wash the feet of disciples and slaves. He humbled himself before those who were his inferiors, but we disdain to be humbled before our equals or often our betters, a fact that arises from no other reason than from our disbelief in the future.[25]

Perhaps the period of mystagogia will be especially marked by preaching that reminds the neophytes and the liturgical assembly of the ongoing consequences of their baptismal commitment. Such preaching will not only encourage but report new patterns of behavior grounded in the gospel and the realities of contemporary living.

Revealing the Future Present

A final approach of initiation preaching in the patristic era is the evocation of the reign of God through participation in liturgical rituals. This eschatological approach tends to be the most neglected in contemporary preaching. It could, however, provide a needed corrective to approaches that concentrate only on historical reconstruction of past religious events or the self-expression of the worshiping assembly at liturgy.

The notion that what is begun in baptismal ritual is brought to completion in the return to Paradise is strongly depicted in a second-century Syriac text originating in Antioch or Edessa, the *Ode of Solomon* 11:

My eyes were enlightened,
and my face received the dew;

And my breath was refreshed
by the pleasant fragrance of the Lord.

And he took me to his Paradise,
wherein is the wealth of the Lord's pleasure.

(I contemplated blooming and fruit-bearing trees,
and self-grown was their crown.

Their branches were flourishing
and their roots were shining;
their roots [were] from an immortal land.

And a river of gladness was irrigating them,
and the region round about them in the land of eternal life.)

Then I adored the Lord because of his magnificence.
And I said, blessed, O Lord, are they
who are planted in your land,
and who have a place in your Paradise;

And who grow in the growth of your trees,
and have passed from darkness into light. . . .

Praise be to you, O God, the delight of Paradise for ever.

Hallelujah.[26]

Notice that the life of heaven is not imaged as "pie in the sky by and by," but as an extension of what has already been experienced in sacramental forms. Would that the warmth of our communities, the integrity of its leadership, the authenticity of its gestures, and the beauty of its song and speech would enrapture participants, giving them a genuine foretaste of the world to come!

Conclusion

The concluding prayer of Gregory of Nyssa's *Homily for the Feast of Lights* not only provides an exquisite example of eschatologically oriented initiation preaching but also a wonderful conclusion for this chapter and this monograph. Note how deftly, in sketching his portrait of paradise, Gregory intertwines images from nature and culture with allusions to biblical narrative and behavioral standards. These rapturous phrases remind us that the goal of liturgical preaching is not simply to inculcate the scriptures, to explicate the rituals or to instruct the congregation; rather, it is to call the entire liturgical assembly to prayerful thanks and praise:

> For you truly, O Lord, are the pure and eternal fount of goodness, who did justly turn away from us, and in loving kindness did have mercy upon us. You did hate, and were reconciled; you did curse, and did bless; you did banish us from Paradise, and did recall us; you did strip off the fig-tree leaves, an unseemly covering, and put upon us a costly garment; you did open the prison, and did release the condemned; you did sprinkle us with clean water, and cleanse us from our filthiness. No longer shall Adam be confounded when called by you, nor hide himself, convicted by his conscience, cowering in the thicket of Paradise. Nor shall the flaming sword encircle Paradise around, and make the entrance inaccessible to those that draw near; but all is turned to joy for us that were the heirs of sin: Paradise, yes, heaven itself may be trodden by [humans]: and the creation, in the world and above the world, that once was at variance with itself, is knit together in friendship: and we [mortals] are made to join in the angels' song, offering the worship of their praise to God. For all these things then let us sing to God that hymn of joy, which lips touched by the Spirit long ago sang loudly: "Let my soul be joyful in the Lord: for he has clothed me with a garment of salvation, and has put upon me a robe of gladness: as on a bridegroom he has set a miter upon me, and as a bride he has adorned me with fair array" [Isaiah 61:10]. And truly the adorner of the bride is Christ, who is, and was, and shall be, blessed now and for evermore. Amen.[27]

Endnotes

Chapter 1

[1]For other approaches to this topic see Reginald H. Fuller, *What is Liturgical Preaching?* Studies in Ministry and Worship, 1 (London: SCM Press, 1957); William Skudlarek, *The Word in Worship: Preaching in a Liturgical Context* (Nashville: Abingdon, 1981); Gerard S. Sloyan, *Worshipful Preaching* (Philadelphia: Fortress, 1984).

[2]"Evangelization is the first and most basic kind of preaching. It is addressed to those, who, for whatever reason, do not yet believe in Jesus. . . . [It] is the preaching of the word of God that aims at giving birth to an internalized faith-trust relationship to the Lord in those who have not yet been converted or who have been only partially converted." John Burke and Thomas P. Doyle, *The Homilist's Guide to Scripture, Theology, and Canon Law* (New York: Pueblo, 1987), 120, 122.

[3]"Catechetical preaching . . . focuses on the living out of the newly professed faith in terms of the customs, tradition, doctrines, and practices of the believing community to which the acceptance of the gospel message has brought the believer." Burke-Doyle, 124.

[4]Burke and Doyle use the term *didascalia* to refer to what I mean by mystagogical preaching: "[D]idascalia signifies that kind of preaching of the word of God that seeks to bring the listener into fullest union with the Father, the Son, and the Holy Spirit. . . . Didascalia nourishes those Christians already mature in faith whom God is calling to a fullness of relationship. It is geared ultimately to fostering nothing less than what has classically been known as mystical union." Burke-Doyle, 125–26.

[5]William H. Willimon, *The Service of God: How Worship and Ethics are Related* (Nashville TN: Abingdon Press, 1983), 151; emphasis added.

[6]For a succinct discussion of the character of a liturgical homily, see Robert P. Wasnak, "Homily," in *The New Dictionary of Sacramental Worship*, ed. Peter E. Fink (Collegeville MN: The Liturgical Press, 1990), 552–58.

[7]Norman Neaves, "Preaching in Pastoral Perspective," in Edmund A. Steimle, Morris J. Niederthal, and Charles Rice, *Preaching the Story* (Philadelphia, PA: Fortress Press, 1980), 111–12.

[8]Susan Howatch, *Mystical Paths* (New York: Fawcett Crest, 1992), 474–75.

ENDNOTES

Chapter 2

[1]The Latin original of *Evangelii nuntiandi* can be found in *Acta Apostolicae Sedis* 68 (1976), 6–76. The English translation of this quotation appears in International Commission on English in the Liturgy, *Documents on the Liturgy 1963–1979: Conciliar, Papal, and Curial Texts* (DOL) (Collegeville MN: The Liturgical Press, 1982), 589–90.

[2]The Latin original of *Catechesi tradendae* can be found in *Acta Apostolicae Sedis* 71 (1979) 1277–1340. The English translation of this quotation appears in DOL, 209.

Chapter 3

[1]O. C. Edwards, *Elements of Homiletic: A Method for Preparing to Preach* (New York: Pueblo, 1982), 22–23.

[2]I. H. Dalmais, "Theology of the Liturgical Celebration," in *The Church at Prayer: An Introduction to the Liturgy. Volume One: Principles of the Liturgy,* new edition, ed. A. G. Martimort, trans. M. J. O'Connell (Collegeville MN: The Liturgical Press, 1987), 229.

[3]Much information on the history of Christian initiation, with a helpful bibliography for further research, is contained in *The Study of Liturgy,* rev. ed., ed. Cheslyn Jones *et al.* (London/New York: SPCK/Oxford University Press, 1992), 111–83.

[4]Edwards, *Elements of Homiletic,* 46.

[5]Charles Harold Dodd, *The Apostolic Preaching and Its Developments* (New York: Harper and Brothers, 1962), 17.

[6]Arndt L. Halvorson, *Authentic Preaching: The Creative Encounter*

Between the Person of the Preacher, the Biblical Text, and Contemporary Life and Literature in Gospel Proclamation (Minneapolis MN: Augsburg Publishing House, 1992), 11.

[7]Walter J. Burghardt, *Tell the Next Generation: Homilies and Near Homilies* (New York/Ramsey: Paulist Press, 1980), 9.

[8]Elisabeth Schüssler Fiorenza in *A New Look at Preaching,* ed. John Burke (Wilmington MD: Michael Glazier, 1983), 45–46.

[9]Tony Kushner, *Angels in America: A Gay Fantasia on National Themes. Part Two: Perestroika* (New York: Theatre Communications Group, Inc., 1994), 77–78.

[10]Thomas H. Troeger, *Imagining a Sermon* (Nashville, TN: Abingdon Press, 1990).

Chapter 4

[1]For representative samples of patristic initiation preaching in English translation see: Thomas M. Finn, *Early Christian Baptism and the Catechumenate: West and East Syria,* Message of the Fathers of the Church, 5 (Collegeville MN: The Liturgical Press, 1992); *idem, Early Christian Baptism and the Catechumenate: Italy, North Africa, and Egypt,* Message of the Fathers of the Church, 6 (Collegeville MN: The Liturgical Press, 1992); Enrico Mazza, *Mystagogy: A Theology of Liturgy in the Patristic Age,* trans. Matthew J. O'Connell (New York: Pueblo Publishing Company, 1989); Hugh M. Riley, *Christian Initiation. A Comparative Study of the Interpretation of the Baptismal Liturgy in the Mystagogical Writings of Cyril of*

Jerusalem, John Chrysostom, Theodore of Mopsuestia, and Ambrose of Milan, The Catholic University of America Studies in Christian Antiquity, 17 (Washington DC: The Catholic University of America Press, 1974); Edward Yarnold, *The Awe-Inspiring Rites of Initiation: Baptismal Homilies of the Fourth Century* (Slough: St. Paul Publications, 1972).

[2]Translation by Stuart G. Hall, *Melito of Sardis: On Pascha and Fragments,* Oxford Early Christian Texts (Oxford: Clarendon, 1979), 73.

[3]Translation by Sebastian Brock, *The Harp of the Spirit: Eighteen Poems of Saint Ephrem,* 2nd ed. enlarged (London: Fellowship of St. Alban and St. Sergius, 1983), 47.

[4]Translation by Roy J. Deferrari, *Saint Ambrose: Theological and Dogmatic Works,* Fathers of the Church, 44 (Washington DC: The Catholic University of America Press, 1963), 290.

[5]Translation adapted from Henry Austin Wilson, "On the Baptism of Christ," in *Gregory of Nyssa: Dogmatic Treatises, etc.,* trans. William Moore and Henry Austin Wilson, *Nicene and Post-Nicene Fathers, Second Series,* 5 (reprint: Peabody, MA: Hendrickson Publishers, Inc., 1994), 519.

[6]Thomas Mary Berry, *Befriending the Earth: A Theology of Reconciliation between Humans and the Earth* (Mystic CT: Twenty-third Publications, 1991).

[7]Brian Swimme and Thomas Berry, *The Universe Story: From the Primordial Flaring Forth to the Ecozoic Era — A Celebration of the Unfolding of the Cosmos* (San Francisco: HarperSan Francisco, 1992).

[8]Sallie McFague, *The Body of God: An Ecological Theology* (Minneapolis: Fortress, 1993).

[9]Translation by Edward Yarnold, *The Awe-Inspiring Rites of Initiation* (Slough: St. Paul Publications, 1972) 195 – 96.

[10]Translation by J. M. Joncas from "Tractatus I 32 (II 30)" in *Zenonis Veronensis Tractatus,* ed. Bengt Löfstedt, Corpus Christianorum Series Latina, 22 (Turnholt: Brepols, 1971) 83.

[11]Translation by Yarnold in *The Awe-Inspiring Rites,* 162 – 63.

[12]Translation by Deferrari, *Saint Ambrose,* 271.

[13]Translation by Mary Sarah Muldowney, *Saint Augustine: Sermons on the Liturgical Seasons,* Fathers of the Church, 38 (Washington DC: The Catholic University Press of America, 1959), 196 – 97.

[14]Translation adapted from Robert W. Thomson, *The Teaching of Saint Gregory: An Early Armenian Catechism,* Harvard Armenian Texts and Studies, 3 (Cambridge MA: Harvard University Press, 1970), 89 – 90.

[15]Translation by Ernest Evans, *Tertullian's Homily on Baptism* (London: SPCK, 1964), 19.

[16]Translation from Leo P. McCauley and Anthony A. Stephenson, *The Works of Saint Cyril of Jerusalem: Volume 2,* Fathers of the Church, 64 (Washington DC: The Catholic University of America Press, 1970), 153 – 54.

ENDNOTES

[17]Translation by Jacob Neusner, *Aphrahat and Judaism: The Christian Jewish Argument in Fourth-Century Iran* (Leiden: Brill, 1971), 29–30.

[18]Translation adapted from Wilson, "Baptism," 524.

[19]Translation from McCauley and Stephenson, *The Works of Saint Cyril of Jerusalem: Volume 2*, 169–70.

[20]Translation by Evans, *Tertullian's Homily on Baptism*, 35.

[21]For more information see James B. Dunning, *Echoing God's Word: Formation for Catechists and Homilists in a Catechumenal Church* (Arlington VA: The North American Forum on the Catechumenate, 1993) 151–74. Dunning acknowledges that he has adapted this framework from John Baldovin, "The Bible and Liturgy, Part One: The State of the Bible Today," *Catechumenate* 11 (September 1989) 12–19.

[22]Late in 1993 the Pontifical Biblical Commission issued an instruction on "Biblical Interpretation in the Church" that discussed various approaches to scripture developed in the last quarter century in addition to the historical-critical model; for an English translation of the document see *Origins* dated 6 January 1994. Eight contemporary approaches to biblical interpretation (historical, canonical, literary, rhetorical, African American, philosophical, theological) are explained and illustrated with sample preaching texts in *Hermeneutics for Preaching: Approaches to Contemporary Interpretations of Scripture*, ed. Raymond Bailey (Nashville TN: Broadman Press, 1992).

[23]Translation by J. M. Joncas from Giuseppe Sobrero, *Anonimo Veronese: omelie mistagogiche e catechetiche. Edizione critica e studio*, Bibliotheca «Ephemerides Liturgicae» «Subsidia», 66, Monumenta Italiae Liturgica, 1 (Roma: C.L.V. Edizioni Liturgiche, 1992), 120.

[24]Translation from Leo P. McCauley and Anthony A. Stephenson, *Cyril of Jerusalem: Catecheses*, Fathers of the Church, 64 (Washington DC: The Catholic University of America Press, 1970), 156–58.

[25]Translation by Joncas from Giuseppe Sobrero, *Anonimo Veronese*, 127–29.

[26]Translation from *The Old Testament Pseudepigrapha*, 2 vols, ed. James H. Charlesworth (Garden City: Doubleday, 1985) II:745–46.

[27]Translation adapted from Wilson, "Baptism," 524.

Annotated Bibliography

1. History of Preaching

Brilioth, Yngve. *A Brief History of Preaching.* Trans. Karl E. Mattson. Philadelphia, PA: Fortress Press, 1965.

Outlines history of (European) Christian preaching. Notes three basic dimensions (liturgical, exegetical, prophetic) linking Jewish and early Christian understandings of preaching. Discusses the Greek homily, Augustine and his era, preaching in the Middle Ages, and Protestant preaching from Luther to Carpzov. Presents an ecumenical survey of preaching on the eve of the Second Vatican Council.

Carroll, Thomas K. *Preaching the Word.* Message of the Fathers of the Church, 11. Wilmington, DE: Michael Glazier, 1984.

An expansion of Brilioth's volume from the New Testament period through Gregory the Great. Contrasts the Greek homily and the Latin sermon with many examples from their patristic practitioners.

Hunter, David G. *Preaching in the Patristic Age: Studies in Honor of Walter J. Brughardt, S.J.* New York-Mahwah: Paulist Press, 1989.

Individual essays on various aspects of the preaching of Origen, Gregory Nazianzus, John Chrysostom, Augustine, Athanasius, Quodvultdeus, and Leo the Great. Survey articles on preaching in the apostolic and subapostolic age, women and patristic preaching, and the use and interpretation of the Bible in early medieval Ireland.

Lisher, Richard. *Theories of Preaching: Selected Readings in the Homiletical Tradition.* Durham, NC: The Labyrinth Press, 1987.

A reader in homiletic theory ranging from ancient Christian writers to those of the twentieth century. Readings in English translation are organized into eight major categories: 1) what is preaching? 2) the preacher, 3) the event of preaching,

4) biblical interpretation in preaching, 5) rhetoric, 6) the hearer, 7) the Holy Spirit, and 8) theology, word and sacrament. A treasure-trove of perspectives and insights.

2. Theory of Preaching

Allmen, Jean-Jacques von. *Preaching and Congregation.* Trans. B. L. Nicholas. Ecumenical Studies in Worship, 10. Richmond, VA: John Knox Press, 1962.

Theses with concise commentary on the "miracle" of preaching, the two "poles" of preaching, the sermon in worship, and sermon preparation from a continental Reformed theologian.

A New Look at Preaching. Ed. John Burke. Good News Studies, 7. Wilmington, DE: Michael Glazier, 1983.

Five major addresses with shorter responses delivered at the First National Ecumenical Scriptural-Theological Symposium on Preaching convened at Emory University by the Word of God Institute to celebrate its 10th anniversary.

Brueggemann, Walter. *Finally Comes the Poet: Daring Speech for Proclamation.* Minneapolis, MN: Fortress, 1989.

The 1989 Lyman Beecher Lectures at Yale Divinity School. Addresses the crisis of interpretation contemporary preachers face from cultural cover stories that dismiss or control the scriptural text and from categories of scripture study that unmask ideological blinders. Calls preachers to be "poets that speak against a prose world" through bringing the text, the baptized, the specific occasion, and a vision of a better world into conversation. Encourages preachers to address topics and emotions often ignored in preaching: numbness and ache, alienation and rage, restlessness and greed, resistance and relinquishment.

Buechner, Frederick. *Telling the Truth: The Gospel as Tragedy, Comedy, and Fairy Tale.* San Francisco, CA: Harper and Row, 1977.

Extraordinary evocation of the preacher's life and task from a master wordsmith and novelist who also serves as an ordained minister.

Burke, John, and Thomas P. Doyle. *The Homilist's Guide to Scripture, Theology and Canon Law.* New York: Pueblo Publishing Company, 1987.

Defines preaching. Highlights church's obligation to preach with its requirements, ministers and offices. Identifies goal of preaching as building Christian community from private spirituality to social transformation. Sketches issues in preaching to contemporary auditors. Applies the foregoing to four "kinds" of preaching: evangelization, catechesis, didascalia, and the liturgical/eucharistic homily. Constructs an "integrated preaching plan" in the final chapter that seems to contradict some of the liturgical principles earlier enunciated in the book.

Buttrick, David. *Homiletic: Moves and Structures.* Philadelphia, PA: Fortress Press, 1987.

The components of a sermon ("moves"): words in narrative contexts, frameworks, images, language, ecclesial context. How these components are structured in preaching: hermeneutical, homiletic, structural and theological theories. Highly recommended.

Chartier, Myron R. *Preaching as Communication: An Interpersonal Perspective.* Nashville, TN: Abingdon, 1981.

Non-technical overview of communication theory (message and process; content, medium and delivery; verbal and nonverbal; oral and written; intentional and unintentional; formal and informal; successful and unsuccessful; levels; sender and receiver; content and relationship) applied to preaching.

Cox, James W. *Preaching.* San Francisco, CA: Harper and Row, 1985.

Professor of Christian Preaching at Southern Baptist Theological Seminary (Louisville, KY) discusses importance of context, content, preparation and delivery in preaching. Emphasizes developing individual preacher's potential and multiple homiletic styles rather than a single pattern.

Craddock, Fred B. *As One Without Authority.* 3rd ed. Nashville, TN: Abingdon, 1979.

Questions "deductive" structuring of sermons: introduction, points, subheads, formal conclusion. Argues for "inductive" structuring in which the form of the sermon interweaves scripture and experience.

_____ . *Preaching.* Nashville, TN: Abingdon, 1985.

Overviews contexts and theology of preaching. Declares that one preaches "something worth saying" through a life of study interpreting the listeners, the text and their interaction.

125

Guides the shaping of "something worth saying" into a sermon by noting the qualities to be sought, its possible forms, the enrichment of the chosen form, and its delivery.

Demaray, Donald E. *An Introduction to Homiletics.* 2nd ed. Grand Rapids, MI: Baker Book House, 1990.

Analyzes the preparation of and disciplines assumed by a preacher. Sketches sermon preparation with remarks on introduction, body, and conclusion. Explores the preaching event. Nine useful "growth sheets" that allow listeners to evaluate the preacher with a view toward development.

Edwards, O. C. *Elements of Homiletic: A Method for Preparing to Preach.* New York: Pueblo Publishing Company, 1982.

Companion volume to Aidan Kavanagh's *Elements of Rite,* both inspired by Strunk and White's classic *Elements of Style.* Bracing directives on interpreting the gospel, applying it to the congregation, developing the preaching idea, constructing (basic outline, filling in, phrasing) and delivering the homily.

Eslinger, Richard L. *A New Hearing: Living Options in Homiletic Method.* Nashville, TN: Abingdon, 1987.

Presents and critiques five prominent 1980s preachers: Charles Rice (storytelling method), Henry Mitchell (black narrative method), Eugene Lowry (narrative and inductive method), Fred Craddock (inductive method) and David Buttrick (phenomenological method). Clear assessment of strengths and weaknesses of each model.

Fichtner, Joseph. *To Stand and Speak for Christ: A Theology of Preaching.* New York: Alba House, 1981.

Reflections arising from a seminar in the theology of preaching taught at Mount St. Mary's Seminary (Emmitsburg, MD). Helpful discussion of Protestant and Catholic understandings of kerygmatic theology.

Fuller, Reginald H. *What is Liturgical Preaching?* Studies in Ministry and Worship, 1. London: SCM Press, 1957.

Ground-breaking essay from an Anglican perspective on the intrinsic connection of preaching and liturgical worship.

Harris, Daniel E., and Edward F. Murphy. *Overtaken by the Word: The Theology and Practice of Preaching.* Denver, CO: Rubicon Publishing, 1990.

Intended as a text in homiletics for Catholic seminarians and a checklist for ordained Catholic preachers. Emphasizes preaching as storytelling. Foundational volume for the Vincentian Preaching Workshops program.

In the Company of Preachers. Ed. Regina Siegfried and Edward Ruane. Collegeville, MN: The Liturgical Press, 1993.

Substantive essays on preaching from the perspectives of liturgical, biblical, historical, systematic, pastoral and spiritual theology by members of the faculty of the Aquinas Institute of Theology. Essays by Quinn, Pozden, Torvend, and Delaplane would be of special interest to the readers of this monograph.

McClure, John S. *The Four Codes of Preaching: Rhetorical Strategies.* Minneapolis, MN: Fortress Press, 1991.

Fascinating application of semiotic theory to the rhetorical strategies involved in developing preaching. Challenges preachers to consider how the scriptural code promotes sacred memory, the semantic code vouches for theological truth, the symbolic code sponsors the congregation's theological worldview, and the cultural code articulates the religious experience of the congregation.

Preaching and the Non-Ordained: An Interdisciplinary Study. Ed. Nadine Foley. Collegeville, MN: The Liturgical Press, 1983.

Papers from a Dominican conference on preaching by the non-ordained held in Columbus, Ohio 8 – 10 October 1982. Especially important background information for non-ordained catechists and others preaching during the various stages of the RCIA.

Skudlarek, William. *The Word in Worship: Preaching in a Liturgical Context.* Nashville, TN: Abingdon, 1981.

Reflections on biblical preaching in the contexts of the liturgical year, the lectionary, eucharist, baptism, matrimony and death by the principal writer of Fulfilled in Your Hearing.

Sloyan, Gerard S. *Worshipful Preaching.* Philadelphia, PA: Fortress Press, 1984.

Serious defence of and call for effective biblical preaching based on the three-year Sunay lectionary cycle.